UPgrade

Course Book

A FIRST COURSE
IN ENGLISH
FOR HIGHER STUDIES

Richard Harrison

Garnet
EDUCATION

Published by

Garnet Publishing Ltd.

8 Southern Court, South Street, Reading RG1 4QS, UK

British Library Cataloguing-in-Publication Data

A catalogue record for this book is available from the British Library.

ISBN 1 85964 705 7

Production

Project manager:	Lucy Thompson
Editorial team:	Richard Peacock, John Bates
Art director:	David Rose
Design:	Janette Hill
Illustration:	Beehive Illustration: Adam Abel, Adrian Barclay, Colin Brown, Janos Jantner, Roger Goode, Andy Keylock; Janette Hill, Doug Nash, Red Giraffe, Karen Rose, Ian West
Photography:	Corbis: Paul Almasy, John Atashian, Bettmann, Brooklyn Productions, Stephane Cardinale/People Avenue, Howard Davies, Rufus F. Folkks, Jose Fuste Raga, Marc Garanger, Alex Gotfryd, Annie Griffiths Belt, So Hing-Keung, Jack Hollingsworth, Hulton-Deutsch Collection, Hurewitz Creative, Reed Kaestner, Charles & Josette Lenars, John Lund, Richard T. Nowitz, PACHA, Jose Luis Pelaez, Inc., Steve Raymer, Roger Ressmeyer, Kim Sayer, Kevin Schafer, John Springer Collection, Steve Starr, Sygma Collection, Peter Turnley, Staffan Widstrand; Getty Images: Adrian Dennis, Susan Greenwood, Matthew Stockman, Bruno Vincent; Digital Vision, Image Source, Jordan Tourism Board, Mirrorpix.com, PhotoDisc, Pixtal, Space Adventures, United Nations
Audio production:	Matinée Sound & Vision Ltd.

'The Future of English' by David Graddol

© The British Council 1997, 2000.

Extracts reproduced by permission of the British Council. All rights reserved.

Every effort has been made to trace the copyright holders and we apologize in advance for any unintentional omissions. We will be happy to insert the appropriate acknowledgements in any subsequent edition.

Printed and bound

in Lebanon by International Press

CONTENTS

BOOK MAP

Unit	Topics/Vocabulary	Language in Focus	Skills in Focus – listening and speaking	Skills in Focus – reading and writing	Study Skills
1 CAMPUS	• campus description and facilities • places where people study • rooms and offices	• greetings and introductions • possessive adjectives	• listening for information • listening to and asking for directions	• reading for specific information • writing e-mails	• learning vocabulary
2 TIME	• clocks and calendars • timetables • days of the week • academic subjects	• telling the time • days of the week • *have/has got* • time phrases	• arranging to meet • discussing timetables	• reading for comprehension • writing about timetables/routines	• getting organised for study
3 AT HOME	• places where people live • lifestyles • food and drink	• present simple • welcoming visitors • *a/some* • apostrophes	• offering food and drink • ordering in a restaurant	• finding information • writing about oneself and others	• learning grammar
4 AROUND THE WORLD	• countries of the world • continents • travel and tourism	• countable/uncountable nouns • *how much/how many* • possessive pronouns	• checking items in a list • giving a short presentation • using tables and charts • ordinal numbers	• transferring information from a text to a chart • making notes from a text • writing about a country	• using a dictionary
5 IN CLASS	• learning styles • classroom furniture • classroom instructions	• imperatives • object pronouns • prepositions of place	• listening to descriptions of places • taking part in a debate	• understanding descriptions of places and objects • writing descriptions of places and objects	• learning words and their collocations

REVIEW UNIT A

Unit	Topics/Vocabulary	Language in Focus	Skills in Focus – listening and speaking	Skills in Focus – reading and writing	Study Skills
6 WORLD CITIES	• information about cities • airports • seasons and climate	• comparative adjectives • question forms – *have/has got, do/does* • asking for information	• giving a short talk • comparing places • taking notes from a talk	• reading for comprehension • writing about a city • letter writing	• using context to guess meaning of words
7 THE WORLD OF COMPUTERS	• computer hardware • using computers • e-mail	• 'wh' questions – present simple tense • *how* and *which* • subject and object questions • asking for and giving help	• explaining how to do something • listening to a radio discussion and making notes • conducting a class survey	• reading for information • writing e-mail addresses • writing e-mails	• asking questions for information/ clarification
8 WORK	• office equipment • job descriptions • communication	• present simple – negative forms • past simple – verb *to be* • telephone language	• listening to a telephone call • taking and leaving messages • giving presentations	• reading for information • writing instructions • writing about people and their work routines	• improving writing

Unit	Topics/Vocabulary	Language in Focus	Skills in Focus – listening and speaking	Skills in Focus – reading and writing	Study Skills
9 FREE TIME	• sports, pastimes and hobbies • weather and natural phenomena	• verb + -ing (love/like/hate/enjoy) • intensifiers (very, quite, extremely, etc.)	• talking about the weather • listening for information • interviewing • giving presentations	• identifying the topic of a paragraph • writing definitions • writing about likes and dislikes	• being a good listener
10 MY WAY	• cultural differences • national holidays and festivals	• adverbs of frequency • describing and asking about routines • sequence markers (first, then, after that, etc.)	• saying the date • listening to a lecture – taking notes • describing festivals and customs	• identifying the topic of a paragraph • writing about festivals • writing about study routines	• taking notes when reading and listening

REVIEW UNIT B

Unit	Topics/Vocabulary	Language in Focus	Skills in Focus – listening and speaking	Skills in Focus – reading and writing	Study Skills
11 INTERNATIONAL ENGLISH	• languages • countries • nationalities • software	• past time phrases • adjectives of nationality • can/can't, could/couldn't • percentages and decimals • making requests	• conducting a survey • listening to a talk – taking notes • discussing the future	• reading an advert • designing a poster • writing a formal letter	• using abbreviations and headings in notes
12 SUMMER VACATION	• flights • hotels • sightseeing	• present continuous • past simple – irregular forms • must/have to • booking a flight	• listening for detail • presenting tourist information • describing a scene	• reading brochures • 'reading between the lines' • writing postcards	• using different sources of information
13 HOW TO STUDY	• learning • memory, intelligence and motivation	• should/ought to • asking for and giving advice • present continuous – questions and negative forms	• listening to a talk – taking notes • taking part in a debate	• ordering paragraphs • writing letters and e-mails	• making notes visual – memory maps
14 FAMOUS NAMES	• fame • personal qualities • life stories • professions	• was/were born • past simple – regular forms • past simple – questions and negatives • comparative and superlative adjectives	• listening to a radio programme for information • researching and presenting information	• reading for information • writing a short biography	• making narrative more interesting
15 WHAT'S NEXT?	• future plans • space travel	• present continuous to express future • going to • will • expressing hopes, wishes and dreams	• listening to a radio interview • role play – interviewing famous people • giving a talk	• reading a newspaper article for information • writing an informal letter • designing an advertisement	• taking an active part in discussions

REVIEW UNIT C

Introduction

Discussion

 1 **Look at the picture of a university campus.**

a) Who are the two men in the picture? What are they studying?

b) Do you like the campus? Would you like to study there? Why/Why not?

c) What is most important in a school, college or university? Put these points in order (1 for the most important).

beautiful gardens ○

modern buildings ○

good canteens ○

enough computers ○

well-trained lecturers ○

other _____ ○

Listening

 2 **Listen to Hassan and Lee and answer the questions.**

a) What's the name of the university?

b) How many students are there?

 **3** **Lee is talking about the main building. Tick (✓) the places you hear.**

Dean's office ○

Computer laboratory ○

Lecture hall ○

Basketball court ○

Classroom ○

Toilets ○

Registration ○

Canteen ○

Reading and vocabulary

 4 **What other places are there in a college or university? Make a list.**

_____

_____

_____

_____

_____

_____

5 **Read this description of the university campus. Complete the paragraph with these words:**

in the middle of   left   behind

right   in front of   near

There are beautiful gardens around the university campus. As you come in the main entrance there is a car park on the ① _____. On the ② _____ is a four-storey building. That is the administration block. ③ _____ the building is a large fountain and ④ _____ it is a small cafeteria. You can see some students sitting here. They are reading or chatting with one another.

On the right, ⑤ _____ the car park, are some tennis courts. ⑥ _____ the campus there is the main teaching block. On top of the building is a clock-tower. You can see the clock from all parts of the campus.

Language in Focus

Greetings and introductions

1 Read and listen to the introduction.

Freda: Hello. I'm Freda. This is my friend Sonia.

Friend: Hello, Sonia. What are you studying?

Sonia: Maths. What about you?

2 In pairs, introduce your partner to other pairs.

A: Hello. I'm … (A). This is my friend … (B).

B: Hello.

C: Hello. How are you?

A/B: Fine/Very well, thanks.

C: I'm … (C). What are you studying?

Listening

3 Listen to these people. Match the recordings to the pictures. Write A, B, C or D in the boxes.

4 Listen to the same people again. Write in the missing words.

A Good _____. My _____ Professor Jack Norman. _____ your new _____ lecturer.

B **1:** Oh, hello, Patricia! _____ are _____ ?

2: Hello, Elsa. I'm _____. It's lovely to _____ you again.

C **1:** Alan, _____ is _____ dean, Dr Mitina.

2: _____ do you _____?

3: _____ to _____ you.

D Good _____. _____ Fatima Saeedi. _____ is the news in English from METV. Here are the headlines.

Thinking about grammar
Possessive adjectives

my   your   our

5 **Complete the introduction.**

Welcome to _____ university. _____ name's
Professor Norman. I'm _____ new Maths
lecturer.

his   her   their

6 **Complete the sentences.**

a) This is our dean – Dr Mitina. And

   that's _____ office.

b) Here are the department secretaries.

   This is _____ office.

c) That's our Maths tutor, Professor
   Norman.

   And this is _____ car.

7 **Write the possessive adjectives:** *my,*
your, our, his, her or *their.*

Guard: Is this ① _____ car, Hassan?

Hassan: No, I haven't got a car. This
belongs to Professor Norman. It's
② _____ car.

Professor Norman: No, it's not ③ _____ car.
It belongs to my wife.

Guard: So it's ④ _____ car.

Mrs Norman: Well, actually, dear, it belongs
to both of us. It's ⑤ _____ car.

Professor Norman: Yes, that's right.

Guard: And what about this Suzuki jeep?

Lee: It belongs to me and my brother, Kim.

Hassan: Yes, that's right. It's ⑥ _____ jeep.

Skills in Focus – listening and speaking

Listening for information

1 Hassan is telling a new student about the Medical Faculty building. Write the names of these rooms on the plan:

library   lecture hall   computer lab
Prof Norman's office   toilets

secretary's office

main door

Listening to directions

2 Rosa is helping a foreign visitor. Where is the Language Centre? Put an X on the map.

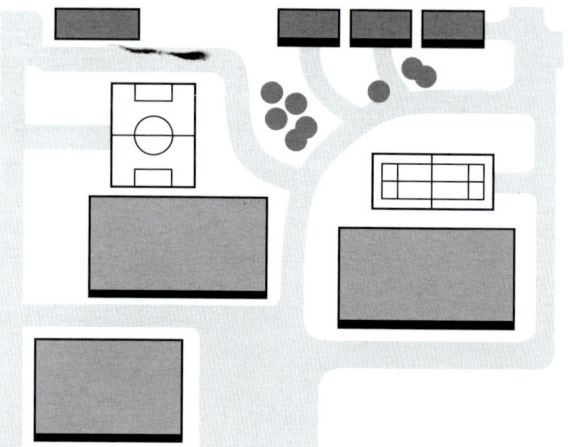

Role play

3 Find a partner and practise the dialogue.

Student A: You are a foreign visitor to the campus.

Student B: You are a student, giving directions to the visitor.

A: Excuse me. Do you speak English?

B: Yes. Can I help you?

A: Yes, please. I'm looking for the Language Centre.

B: It's over there in the main building, on the ground floor.

A: Thanks very much.

4 Now make similar dialogues.

A Ask for directions to other places on the campus. For example:

the computer room
Registration
Mr Wilkinson's office
the canteen
the bookshop

B Give directions to your partner. Use these phrases:

It's   over there …
      near the …
      next to …
      on the right/left
      on the ground/first floor, etc.

El Dorado? It's over there. Behind the mountain.

Skills in Focus – reading and writing

Reading for information

 1 Find information from the Millennium University prospectus to complete the table.

	Yes	No
a) Does the university have courses in business?	✓	○
b) Can students live on campus?	○	○
c) Does the university have short courses?	○	○
d) Is it located in a city?	○	○
e) Do you need good English to study there?	○	○
f) Does the university have a website?	○	○

2 Here is some information about the university from the prospectus. Choose the correct heading for each piece of information from the box.

location   students   qualifications
name   sports facilities
medium of instruction   faculties

The Millennium University
near Exeter, in south-west England
8,000
7
gymnasium, swimming pools, basketball and tennis courts, football pitches, athletics track
English
Master's and Bachelor's degrees, diplomas, certificates

The Millennium University

Welcome to the Millennium University. It is a new English-medium university for students from all over the world. It was opened by the Secretary-General of the United Nations in the year 2000.

The main campus is located in the countryside of southwest England, about 20 kilometres west of the city of Exeter. It has more than 8,000 students from nearly 50 different countries. We offer the most up-to-date teaching facilities, well-qualified staff and a beautiful campus. If you want to stay on the campus, we have accommodation for more than 3,000 students.

The university has seven faculties: Law, Science, Arts, Engineering, Science, Education and Business Studies. There is also a fully equipped Language Centre, an Information Technology Centre, a large library and many computer laboratories. Our sports facilities are the best in the United Kingdom. As well as a gymnasium, we have swimming pools, basketball and tennis courts, football pitches and an athletics track.

The medium of instruction is English, and every student must be able to speak and write English to a high standard. Overseas students must pass an entry test in English before they can start their studies. They should also study another foreign language. The university offers different types of qualifications at Master's, Bachelor's and diploma levels. It also offers short certificate courses.

If you would like more information on the courses we offer at the Millennium University, why not visit our website?

 3 Make a similar table with information about the place where you study, then write a paragraph for a prospectus.

Reading and writing

 4 **Read the message below.**

   a) Where is Parween at the moment?
   b) Where is she from?
   c) Has she ever used e-mail before?
   d) Do you think she is happy at college?

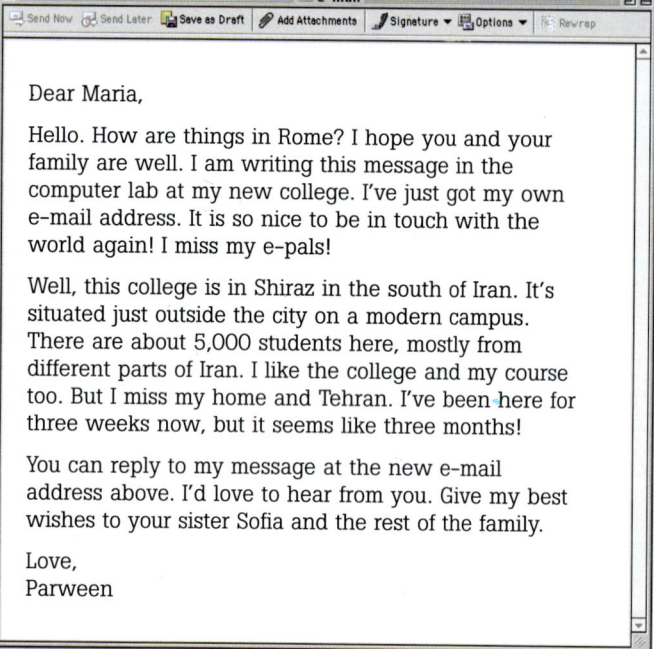

Dear Maria,

Hello. How are things in Rome? I hope you and your family are well. I am writing this message in the computer lab at my new college. I've just got my own e-mail address. It is so nice to be in touch with the world again! I miss my e-pals!

Well, this college is in Shiraz in the south of Iran. It's situated just outside the city on a modern campus. There are about 5,000 students here, mostly from different parts of Iran. I like the college and my course too. But I miss my home and Tehran. I've been here for three weeks now, but it seems like three months!

You can reply to my message at the new e-mail address above. I'd love to hear from you. Give my best wishes to your sister Sofia and the rest of the family.

Love,
Parween

5 **Complete the message below to Parween with the words in the box. Use a computer if you can.**

> Shiraz   my   miss   your   like
> reply   message   great

Hi Parween,

Thanks for _____ e-mail _____. It was _____ to

hear from you again. I'm glad that you _____ your

college in _____. I'm sure that your family and

friends in Tehran _____ you very much, too. Please

_____ to _____ message soon!

Maria

 6 **You are one of Parween's 'e-pals'. Write your own message to her.**

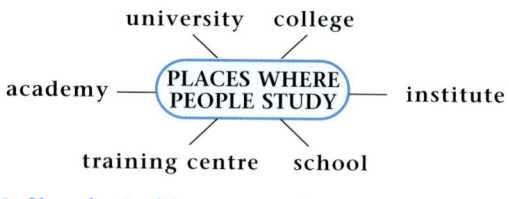

Study Skills and Review

Study Tip | Learning words

- When you learn a word, learn other words that are in the same group.

  For example: **university** belongs to the group 'Places where people study'.

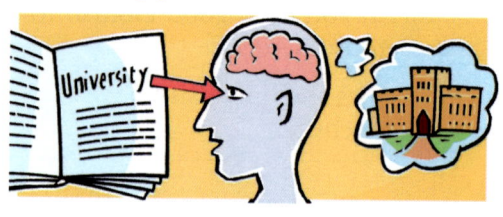

- Your brain likes pictures! Make a drawing. It will help you to remember the word.

1 Make a similar sketch (a spidergram) to the one above. Find words in the group *places where people eat.*

PLACES WHERE PEOPLE EAT

2 Find four words or phrases in the unit that you want to remember. Write them below.

_____ _____

_____ _____

3 Now make a drawing for each word or write a sentence.

Puzzle: What's this word?

+ us

Vocabulary Review

1 Complete these groups with words from the unit and other words you know. You can write the translation on the right.

Places where people study

English	translation
university	
college	

Places in a college or university

English	translation
lecture hall	
office	
library	

Grammar Review

• Possessive adjectives

singular	plural
my computer	our computer
your computer	your computer
his/her computer	their computer

singular	plural
its	their

Task 1: Choose four possessive adjectives from the table. Write sentences to show the meaning.

For example:

Thailand is a state in Southeast Asia. Its capital is Bangkok.

Language Review

• Greetings and introductions
informal/friendly

Hello/Hi. I'm …
This is my friend …
How are you?
I'm fine/very well, thanks.

more formal

My name's …
I'd like you to meet …
How do you do?
I'm pleased to meet you.

• Other greetings

Good morning.
Good afternoon.
Good evening.

• Asking for and giving directions

Can I help you?
I'm looking for …
Where is … ?

It's over there.
next to …
near …
on the right/on the left …
behind/in front of …
at the end of …
opposite …
between … and …
on the ground/first/second/third floor …

Task 2: Write three sentences giving directions.

For example:

The library is in the main building, next to the computer laboratory.

Introduction

Discussion

 Look at the pictures and discuss the questions in small groups.

a) What do these instruments measure?

b) What are the differences between a clock, a watch and a calendar?

c) How are modern clocks and watches different from these ancient ones?

A

B

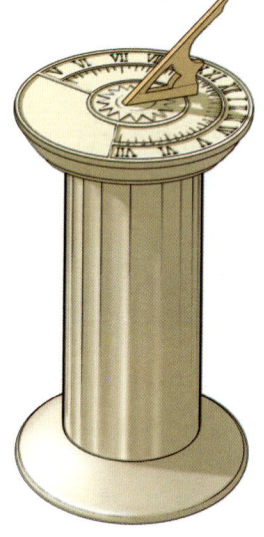

C

Reading

2 Match these descriptions with pictures A, B and C. Write the names of the instruments in the spaces.

@ Ancientclocks.com – Ancient clocks

Back Forward Stop Refresh Home AutoFill Print Mail

Address: @ http://www.ancientclocks.com/ › go

@ Live Home Page @ Apple Computer @ Apple Support @ Apple Store @ Microsoft MacTopia @ MSN »

A Some ancient clocks used water to measure time. In a water clock the water passes through a small hole and collects in a bowl or barrel. There are marks on the sides of the bowl that show the hours. Other water clocks have got 'floats' which rest on the surface of the water. They indicate the time as the water rises.

B Another ancient instrument for measuring time is the hourglass. The glass is shaped into two equal halves and there is a small hole in the centre. When the glass is turned over, sand escapes through the hole. It takes exactly an hour for all the sand to pass through the hole.

C A sundial was one of the first ways of measuring time. It consists of a dial divided into hours and it has got a vertical pointer in the middle. As the sun moves across the sky, the shadow of the pointer falls across the dial and shows the time.

1 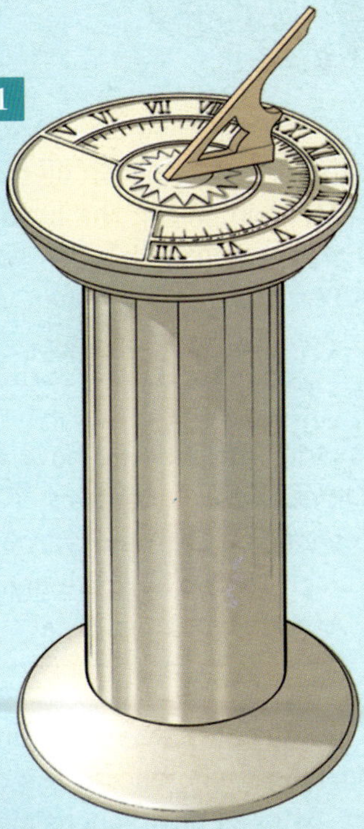
2 
3

Internet zone

Listening

3 Listen to the telephone conversation about a watch. Tick the words you hear.

hand	○	hour	○
strap	○	minute	○
second	○	digital	○
date	○	analogue	○
dial	○	battery	○

Speaking

4 Describe your watch to a partner. Use these phrases:

It's got …   It has …

Language in Focus

Telling the time

1 Listen to people talking about time. Match the six times you hear with the clocks and watches below.

A B C D E F

What's the time?

It's five o'clock.

It's half past seven.

It's seven thirty.

It's (a) quarter to eight.

It's seven forty-five.

It's (a) quarter past ten.

It's ten fifteen.

It's ten past eight.

It's eight ten.

2 In pairs, ask and tell the time. Use these pictures.

Timetables

3 Listen and repeat the days of the week.

Monday   Wednesday   Friday

Tuesday   Thursday   Saturday   Sunday

4 Rosa is talking about her new timetable.

a) Look at the timetable and fill in the days of the week.

b) Read what Rosa says and fill in her timetable for Tuesday and Wednesday.

This is my timetable. As you can see, it's very full.

On Monday I've got English all morning. In the afternoon, after the lunch break, we go to the computer lab for two hours of Computer Studies. And then, at three o'clock, I have an hour of Law.

On Tuesday morning we have Business Management for two hours. Then we've got Economics. In the afternoon, from one o'clock to two, I go to my Spanish class. After that I am free!

Then on Wednesday we've got English in the morning from nine to ten and then Computer Studies until lunchtime. In the afternoon we have Accounting from one o'clock to two and then two hours of English in the language lab.

c) Listen to Rosa. Fill in her timetable for Thursday and Friday. Choose from the subjects in the box.

Business Management   Accounting
English   Law
Finance   Mathematics
Computer Studies   Economics
Physics   Education
Spanish   Marketing

	Monday				
9–10	English				
10–11	English				
11–12	English				
12–1	L U N C H B R E A K				
1–2	Computer Studies				
2–3	Computer Studies				
3–4	Law				

Thinking about grammar
have/has got

5 **Read these examples and underline the verbs.**

a) Mark has got English on Monday morning.

b) The college has got a new computer lab.

c) On Wednesday we have got Spanish and Computer Studies.

d) Listen! I've got a good idea!

e) Elena and Olga have got a problem.

6 **Complete the table below.**

I		We	
You	**have got**	You	**have got**
He/She/It		They	

Negatives:

It has got a leather strap. It **hasn't got** a plastic strap.

We have got Computer Studies tomorrow. We **haven't got** Mathematics.

Note: We can use *have* or *has* in place of *have got* and *has got*.

It **has** a leather strap.

We **have** Computer Studies tomorrow.

7 **Complete the sentences with *have* or *has*.**

a) Sarah _____ got a bad cold.

b) _____ you got the time?

c) We _____ got our French class now.

d) My car _____ got air-conditioning.

e) They _____ got a problem.

f) Our college _____ got a large campus.

g) Mike _____ got a new car.

h) Hurry up! You _____ got an exam!

Prepositions: on, in, at

I'll see you **on** Monday.

Let's meet **at** nine o'clock.

I'm busy **in** the morning.

We're **on** holiday tomorrow!

ON + day

AT + time
+ night/midday/midnight

IN + the morning/afternoon/evening

8 **Complete the dialogue with words from the box.**

tomorrow   morning   on   at   in   week

A: I'd like to see you one day this _____.

B: OK. What about _____?

A: I'm afraid I'm busy all day tomorrow. But I'm free _____ Wednesday.

B: _____ the afternoon? Is that possible?

A: The _____ is better. What about ten o'clock?

B: I've got a meeting _____ ten. Shall we say eleven?

A: Fine.

B: See you then!

Skills in Focus – listening and speaking

Listening for information

 a) Lee is talking to Antonio. They want to meet for a coffee. Listen and find out when and where they arrange to meet.

b) Listen to Jane and Sarah. When and where will they meet for tea?

c) Look at the dialogue below. Listen again and fill in the missing phrases.

Jane: Hello?

Sarah: Hi, Jane. This is Sarah.

Jane: Hi. How are you?

Sarah: I'm fine. And you? I haven't seen you for ages.

Jane: I'm very well.

Sarah: Good. ① _____ for tea one day.

Jane: Tomorrow?

Sarah: I can't tomorrow. ② _____ an exam in the morning. ③ _____ Tuesday?

Jane: I've got volleyball practice in the morning. ④ _____ the afternoon?

Sarah: OK. Three o'clock?

Jane: ⑤ _____ quarter to?

Sarah: Right. Quarter to three. In the canteen?

Jane: No, it's too noisy. ⑥ _____ in the snack bar.

Sarah: That's great. I'll see you on Tuesday.

Jane: At two forty-five.

Sarah: See you then.

Jane: Bye.

Role play

 Make a weekly plan on the diary page below.

October
7th
8th
9th
10th
11th
12th
13th

 Work in pairs. Phone your partner and arrange a time and place to meet. Use these phrases:

A: Let's meet on …
What about … ?
Shall we say … ?

B: Sorry. I've got (a) …
I'm afraid I'm busy.
But I'm free on …

Skills in Focus – reading and writing

Reading

1 **Which of these statements do you agree with? Discuss in a group.**

a) I think a watch should be beautiful and nice to wear.

b) I want a watch that is modern and can do many things.

c) I just want a simple watch that will tell the time accurately.

d) I like to wear a very expensive watch to show my friends.

2 **Read the article about watches. Are these sentences true or false? Correct the false sentences.**

a) Pocket watches came after wristwatches.

b) Some people wear watches like jewellery.

c) Digital watches have got hands to show the time.

d) An alarm is a function of some digital watches.

e) Some watches use atomic energy.

f) In the future, watches may connect to the Internet.

3 **Find these words in the text. What do they mean?**

> fashion   jewellery   vibrate
> accurate   tiny   function

TIME FOR A NEW WATCH?

Watches, unlike clocks, are designed for carrying around. The first watches were carried in the pocket or fixed to a belt. Later came the 'wristwatch' that we use today. As well as a time-piece, it is also a fashion item, like jewellery.

There are two types of watch. Watches that use hands and a dial to show the time are called analogue watches. They have one hand to show hours and another to show the minutes past, or to, the hour. Sometimes they also have a third hand that shows seconds.

Other watches use numbers to show the time, for example 15.35. These are called digital watches. They are very accurate.

Many modern watches use batteries. They also have tiny quartz crystals inside. These crystals vibrate 100,000 times a second. They are very accurate. Some digital watches are like tiny computers. They have many different functions, such as built-in alarms and stopwatches.

In the future, watches may not have batteries or crystals inside them. They may use the sun, atomic energy or even the heat of your own body for power. They may also have new functions. For example, we may be able to connect to the Internet using our watches. We may also use our watches to make videophone calls to people on the other side of the world. Will watches really become like computers and mobile phones? Only time will tell.

Reading and writing

 4 **Read Kim's e-mail message to Maria.**

   a) How many hours of English has Kim got in a week?

   b) How many subjects does she study?

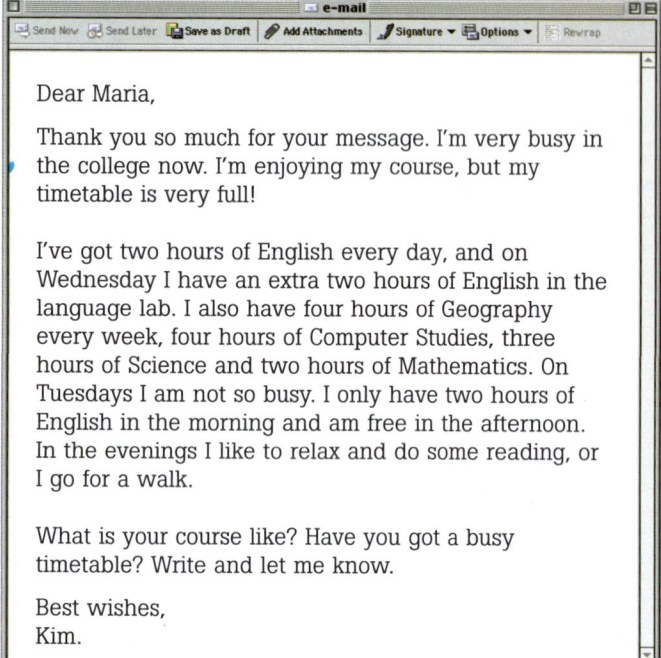

Dear Maria,

Thank you so much for your message. I'm very busy in the college now. I'm enjoying my course, but my timetable is very full!

I've got two hours of English every day, and on Wednesday I have an extra two hours of English in the language lab. I also have four hours of Geography every week, four hours of Computer Studies, three hours of Science and two hours of Mathematics. On Tuesdays I am not so busy. I only have two hours of English in the morning and am free in the afternoon. In the evenings I like to relax and do some reading, or I go for a walk.

What is your course like? Have you got a busy timetable? Write and let me know.

Best wishes,
Kim.

5 **Write a reply to Kim. Tell her about your course and your timetable. Write about 120 words.**

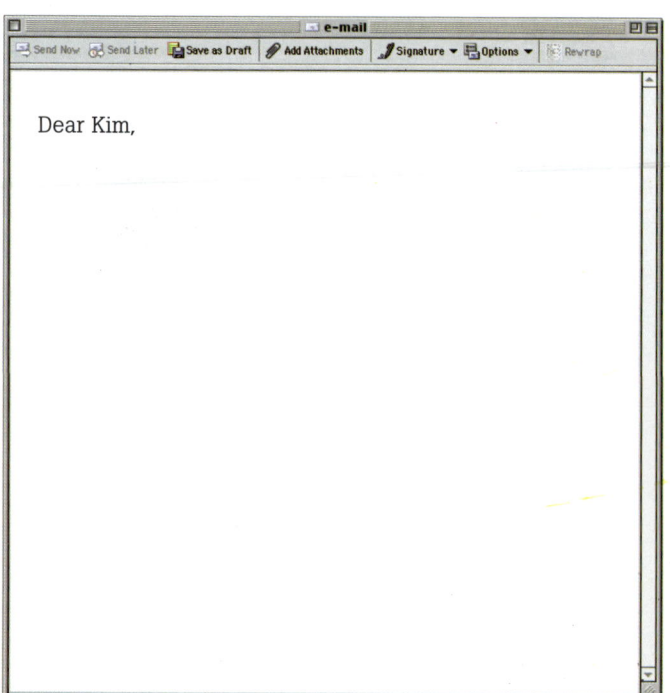

Dear Kim,

Study Tip | Get organised!

A good student is an organised student. Here are some of the things you need.

- A timetable (for your course)
- A study plan (for your private study)
- A quiet place to study (your room, library, etc.)
- Reference and course books
- A list of other resources (computer lab, Internet access, language lab, videos, etc.)
- Help and advice (teachers, tutors, etc., who can help you)

1 **Make a study timetable. First put in all your classes and lectures. Then add times for private study. Also add times when you can use computer labs and language labs.**

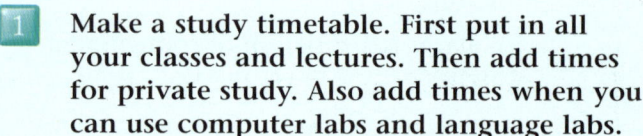

Mon	Tues	Wed	Thurs	Fri	Sat	Sun

2 **Make a list of all the books you need for your studies (course books, grammar books, dictionaries, etc.). Add magazines, journals, Internet sites, videos and cassettes to your list of resources.**

_____

_____

_____

_____

_____

_____

_____

Vocabulary Review

Days of the week

1 Complete the list.

Monday, _____, Wednesday,

_____, Friday, _____, Sunday

Subjects

2 Put these subjects in alphabetical order, then continue the list.

Business Management, Accounting, English,

Law, Finance, Computer Studies, Economics,

Physics, Education, Spanish, Marketing

_____

_____

Time

3 Complete the spidergram.

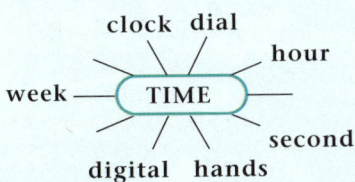

clock   dial

hour

week —— TIME

second

digital   hands

Grammar Review

- *have/have got*

singular	plural
I have (not) got	We have (not) got
You have (not) got	You have (not) got
He/She has (not) got	They have (not) got
It has (not) got	

Note these contractions:

singular	plural
I've, you've, he's, she's, it's got	we've, you've, they've got
haven't, hasn't got	haven't got

Task 1: Write four sentences about your course or your place of study. Use *have(n't)/has(n't) got.*

For example:

We've got French and Chemistry on Tuesday.

Our college is small. It hasn't got many students.

Language Review

- **Asking and telling the time**

What's the time?   Have you got the time?

What time is it?   What time do you make it?

It's (nearly/about/just before/just after) …

I make it …

analogue		digital	
Half past six		Six thirty	06:30
Quarter past six		Six fifteen	06:15
Quarter to six		Five forty-five	05:45
Ten o'clock		Ten	10:00

- **Time phrases**

in	the morning, the afternoon, the evening January, February, etc. the summer, the winter, etc. 1999
at	ten o'clock, half past three, etc. night, midday, midnight
on	Saturday, Sunday, Monday, etc. holiday

- **Arranging to meet**

Let's meet on Monday.
What about nine thirty?
Shall we say nine forty-five?

Sorry. I've got a meeting.
I'm afraid I'm busy on Monday morning.
But I'm free in the afternoon.

Task 2: Two people are arranging to meet. Write the dialogue with a partner.

Introduction

Discussion

1. **Read the expressions about home. What do they mean?**

   "Home is where the heart is."

   "East, west, home is best."

   "Make yourself at home."

   "It's a home from home."

   "Home sweet home."

   "There's no place like home."

2. **Discuss these pictures. Where are the people from? What is special about their homes?**

Reading

3 **Read the descriptions and match them with the pictures on page 22.**

1) The McLoughlin family are Gypsies. They live in a caravan in Ireland. Hundreds of Gypsies live like that. They travel around the country and work in different places. They usually find seasonal work on farms. Some Gypsies live in houses and send their children to school, but many like the life on the open road.

2) These Bedouin are from Petra in Jordan. They live in a tent which is made of goat and sheep hair. Bedouin tents are usually black or dark brown in colour. In the winter they are warm and in the summer they give protection from the hot desert sun. But life in the desert can be hard and now many Bedouin live in towns.

3) In Brunei, many people live in 'water villages'. The houses are wooden and are built on long legs, so that they are above the level of the river. People do everything in these houses: they wash, cook, eat and sleep. There are also schools and medical clinics in these villages. People walk from one part of the village to another on walkways over the river.

4 **Look carefully at the pictures below. Which four countries do they show?**

Listening

5 **These four people are talking about their homes and families.**

Listen and complete the table. Put ticks (✓) in the boxes.

Nadia

Sam

Sonia

Sergei

A	B	C	D	
				lives in a flat.
				lives in a wooden house.
				has six children.
				is a factory manager.
				speaks five languages.
				studies Mathematics.
				has got a small shop.
				works in a bank.

Language in Focus

Thinking about grammar
Present simple

1 Look at these sentences. Underline the verbs.

a) I live in Aswan in Egypt.

b) Sonia speaks five languages.

c) My son studies English in school.

d) We live in an apartment in Mexico City.

e) Sam works on a farm.

f) Gypsies travel around the country and work in different places.

The verbs are all in the present simple tense.

2 Complete the table using two of the verbs above.

I	live	He	lives
You	work	She	_____
We	study	It	_____
They	speak		

3 Choose the correct form of the verb.

a) My sister *lives/live* in a small house near the sea.

b) We *speak/speaks* Portuguese in Brazil.

c) Kim *work/works* in a factory in Beijing.

d) Many Gypsies *live/lives* in caravans.

e) Anthony *study/studies* French and Philosophy.

f) I only *speak/speaks* two languages – Urdu and English.

g) Two of my brothers *work/works* on a farm.

h) You *study/studies* at Cairo University, don't you?

Welcoming visitors

4 Listen to Jack and Antonio. Complete the conversation with phrases from the box.

> something to drink . Have a seat
> I'm very thirsty   It looks delicious
> Make yourself at home   I'd like some
> Here you are

Jack: Hi.

Antonio: Hello, Jack. It's nice to see you again. ① _____.

Jack: Here?

Antonio: Anywhere. ② _____.

Jack: Thanks.

Antonio: Would you like ③ _____?

Jack: Yes, please. ④ _____. It's really hot today. Have you got cola?

Antonio: No. I've got lemonade or orange juice.

Jack: ⑤ _____ orange juice, please.

Antonio: Just a minute … Right. ⑥ _____.

Jack: That's great. Thanks.

Antonio: Have a piece of cake. Help yourself. My girlfriend made it.

Jack: No, thanks. ⑦ _____, but I'm not very hungry.

Antonio: OK. Now tell me your news.

Jack: Well, do you remember that project … ?

Thinking about grammar
a/an/some

Look at these sentences.

I'd like **a** cup of coffee.

I'd like **some** milk.

Would you like **a** biscuit or **an** apple?

Would you like **some** biscuits?

Would you like **some** juice?

- Nouns such as *biscuit, apple, cup* are countable – *one* biscuit, *two* biscuits … *some* biscuits.

- Nouns such as *milk, juice, water* are uncountable. We say '*some* milk'. We don't say '*two* milks', '*three* waters'.

Food and drink

 Match the words with the pictures below.

sandwiches	a glass of milk
a cake	ice-cream
a cup of coffee	a mug of tea
biscuits	a glass of orange juice
fruit	chocolates
cheese	

6 Divide these nouns into two groups: countable and uncountable. Write them in the table. Add *s, es* or *ies* to the countable nouns.

biscuit   milk   water   country   air
orange   house   oil   computer
college   money   diploma   information
car   traffic   rice

Countable: *a/an/some*	Uncountable: *some*
biscuit(s)	milk

Punctuation

 Put apostrophes (') in these sentences.

a) Im from Rabat in Morocco.

b) My brothers got a new car.

c) Weve got an English lesson this afternoon.

d) Andys a student in the Engineering Faculty.

e) Wed like some apple juice, please.

f) Theyre from Petra in Jordan.

g) Whats the time, please?

h) Id like you to meet Professor Norman.

---

would like

Would you like some tea?

I'd like some coffee.

And Tom?

I think he'd like some coffee, too.

I You He/She/It We They	'd like (would like)	some water.

Skills in Focus – listening and speaking

Role play

1 Practise in pairs or small groups. Offer food and drink to your partner(s).

A: Would you like … ?

Have …

Help yourself to … .

B: Yes, please. (I'm hungry/thirsty.)

I'd like a/some … (It looks/They look delicious!)

No, thanks. (I'm not hungry/thirsty.)

Listening

2 Study the menu. Are there any new words? Check the meanings with a partner. Use a dictionary to help you.

Joe's Diner

Sandwiches:
- ☐ chicken
- ☐ beef
- ☐ tuna
- ☐ cheese
- ☐ egg

Snacks:
- ☐ pizza
- ☐ burger and french fries
- ☐ chicken and french fries
- ☐ salad

Dessert:
- ☐ ice-cream
- ☐ fruit salad
- ☐ apple pie
- ☐ yoghurt

Drinks:
- ☐ tea
- ☐ coffee
- ☐ apple juice
- ☐ orange juice
- ☐ milk
- ☐ milkshake
- ☐ cola
- ☐ lemonade

3 Listen to some customers in a restaurant. What food do they order? Tick (✓) their choices on the menu. (C1/2 = customer 1/2; W = waiter)

4 Listen to part of the conversation again. Complete it with phrases from the box.

> Yes, I'll have   I'd like   We've got
> I'm afraid not   Have you got
> What would you like   Would you like
> And for you, madam   And for you, sir

C1: Yes, yes, I see. Now …

W: ① _____ to have?

C1: Er … I'd like a sandwich to start with.

W: A sandwich. ② _____ beef, tuna, chicken, egg …

C1: I'll have chicken.

W: One chicken sandwich. ③ _____?

C2: ④ _____ a pizza, please, with some salad.

W: So, one pizza and one salad. ⑤ _____ a dessert?

C2: ⑥ _____ some ice-cream, please.

W: We've got strawberry, vanilla, tropical delight, banana …

C2: Strawberry.

W: Strawberry. ⑦ _____?

C1: ⑧ _____ chocolate ice-cream?

W: No, ⑨ _____. Only strawberry …

Skills in Focus – reading and writing

Reading

1 **Discuss these questions in groups.**

a) Do you live in a flat (apartment) or a house?

b) Which is better? Why?

c) How do you usually spend the summer?

2 **Read a Russian student's composition about *dachas* and find answers to these questions.**

a) What is a *dacha*?

b) Where do most Russians live in the winter?

c) Where do many of them live in the summer?

d) Why is the spring a busy time for the owners of *dachas*?

3 **Read the text again. What are the advantages of *dachas*? What are the disadvantages? Make two lists. Include your own ideas.**

advantages	disadvantages

4 **Choose five words from the text that you want to learn.**

Dachas

Most people in Russia live and work in big cities. If you go to any Russian city, you will see tall, grey, concrete buildings around the city centre. People live in flats in these buildings. The flats are usually quite small, with just one or two bedrooms for a family.

During the cold Russian winter these buildings are warm. They have good central heating. However, Russia also has quite hot summers. Because of this, many people leave their flats in the cities and go to live in their dachas.

Dachas are best described as country cottages, small wooden houses built in the country near to the cities. They are normally very basic and do not have the comforts of the city flats. Children usually spend the whole summer there in order to get fresh air and exercise. If their parents are working in the city, there are grandparents or other relatives to look after the children. In the country, they play sports, swim in lakes and rivers or look for mushrooms in the forest.

Each dacha has got a small garden. Most people grow fruit and vegetables for their families and friends. If times are difficult, they can sell these products in the cities. As a result, spring is a very busy time for the owners of the dachas. They make any repairs after the winter snows and frosts, and also prepare the garden for planting.

At the end of the summer, the temperature begins to fall and everyone goes back to the city. Children start school again and parents who were on holiday return to their jobs. Unfortunately, dachas haven't got good heating and are very cold in winter, so Russians are quite happy to be back in their warm flats.

Reading and writing

5 Read about these people. What do they want to do when they finish their studies?

My name's Aysha. I am from Kuala Lumpur in Malaysia. I am a student at the New International University in Alumnia, where I study Physics, Mathematics and Chemistry. However, I don't live on the university campus.

I live in a flat in the centre of Lobono, the capital, with my parents and Sarah, my younger sister. When I leave university I'd like to be a scientific researcher in my home country. I speak two languages: Malay and English. I also understand Chinese, but I don't speak it very well.

My older brother's name is Mike. He comes from Darwin, in the north of Australia. At the moment he's a student at the New International University in Alumnia, where he studies Business Management. He lives in a large house in the suburbs of Lobono, which he shares with five other students. Mike doesn't want to go back to Australia when he leaves university. He says he wants to work for a multinational company in Japan. He speaks three languages: English, French and Japanese.

6 Underline the verbs in each paragraph. What tenses are the verbs? Three of the verbs are in their negative form. Which are they?

7 Now write a paragraph (80 words) about yourself. Where do you live? What languages do you speak? Where do you study (or work)? Use verbs from the unit: *study, live, work, have, be, like, want,* etc.

8 Write a paragraph about someone you know. Remember to use the correct verb forms: *studies, lives, works, has, is/are, likes, wants,* etc.

1 Look at the essay on *dachas*.

a) Find two examples of the word *usually*.

b) What can you see about the position of *usually* in the sentence? Can you make a rule?

2 Now read the texts about Gypsies and Bedouin at the beginning of the unit again.

a) Find two more examples of *usually*. Check your rule.

b) *Usually* is an adverb of frequency. Find out about other adverbs of frequency. Use a grammar book.

Vocabulary Review

Drinks

 Complete the spidergram.

Make spidergrams for:

a) Fruit

b) In a restaurant

Verbs

 Add some more examples to this list of verbs from the unit.

to play　　＿＿＿＿＿＿　　＿＿＿＿＿＿

to grow　　＿＿＿＿＿＿　　＿＿＿＿＿＿

to walk　　＿＿＿＿＿＿　　＿＿＿＿＿＿

to travel　＿＿＿＿＿＿　　＿＿＿＿＿＿

to sell　　＿＿＿＿＿＿　　＿＿＿＿＿＿

Write six example sentences for the verbs.

Grammar Review

- ### Present simple – verb *to live*

 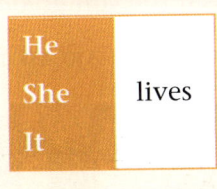

Amir **lives** in a large house in Malaysia.

My parents **live** in a small flat in the suburbs.

- ### Countable/uncountable nouns

countable		uncountable
a/an	*some* (plural)	*some*
biscuit	biscuits	water
apple	apples	milk
sandwich	sandwiches	juice
banana	bananas	cheese

I'd like **a banana**, please.

Have you got **an apple**?

Have **some sandwiches**.

I'll have **some cheese**. It looks delicious.

Task 1: Find five more countable nouns and five uncountable nouns. Choose words which are not in this unit.

Language Review

- ### Offering food and drink

Would you like something to drink?

What would you like to eat/drink?

Have some cake.

Have a biscuit.

Help yourself to some wine.

- ### Saying 'yes' and saying 'no'

Yes, please. (I'm thirsty./I'm hungry.)

No, thank you. (I'm not thirsty./I'm not hungry.)

- ### Requesting

I'd like …

I'll have …

Have you got any … ?

Task 2: A visitor comes to your home. Write a dialogue between you and the visitor. Offer food and drink.

Introduction

Discussion

1 **Some students from the New International University are looking at pictures of their countries. Discuss these questions in small groups.**

a) Where are the places in the photos?

b) Would you like to go there? Why/why not?

c) Think of a title for each picture.

d) What are the advantages of holidaying abroad? What are the disadvantages?

Stand in the middle of the square and look around. Admire the architecture of the buildings, but also feel the sense of history. All the _____ and _____ life of the country is represented here.

Where can you find snow on the Equator? The answer is 3,000 metres above sea level on the top of Kilimanjaro. Meanwhile, down on the plains, you will find _____ animals and _____ jungle.

While you are there, why not take the lift to the viewing platform 120 metres above the ground? You can have a meal in the restaurant and enjoy _____ views of the whole city at the same time.

Swim before breakfast. Then visit the local market and meet the _____ people of the island. Explore by jeep in the afternoon. In the evening eat _____ lobster and watch the sun go down over the ocean. What more could you ask for?

Welcome to the most _____ shopping street in the world! Join the crowds of shoppers looking for bargains. There are shops to suit all tastes here – from the _____ and expensive to the _____.

Reading

2 Read the texts under the pictures. They are from travel brochures. Complete the texts with adjectives from the box.

> political   wonderful   fresh
> tropical   friendly   wild   elegant
> famous   economical   religious

Listening

3 Now listen to the students. They are talking about the places in the pictures. Match the people with pictures A–E.

1 Monica ___

2 Victor ___

3 Sara ___

4 Robert ___

5 Sam ___

Travel vocabulary

4 Look at the map of the world.

a) Mark the continents on the map.
   Africa, America, Asia, Europe, Australasia

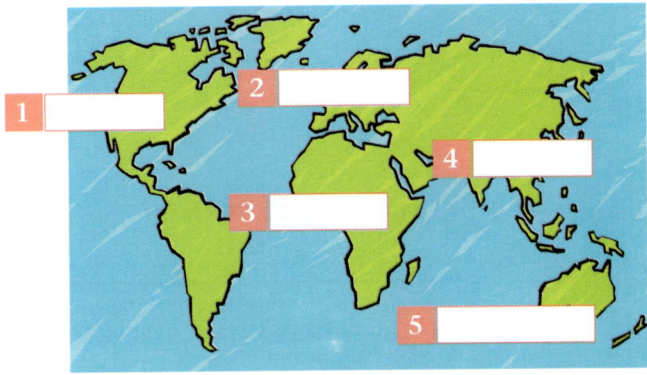

b) Where are the five places from the photos?

5 Match the pictures with the names of types of luggage in the box.

> bag   suitcase   briefcase   box
> handbag   backpack

6 Look at the airport signs and scenes. Where would you see them?

31

Language in Focus

Listening

1 Nina (N) is speaking to a customs officer (CO). Complete the dialogue below with Nina's answers from the box.

> Six bottles. They're presents.
> Two hundred.   Thanks.   Perfume.
> Three.   Yes, it's mine.   Yes, of course.
> Yes – in this bag.

> How many suitcases have you got?

CO: Is this your luggage, madam?

N: ① _____ .

CO: How many suitcases have you got?

N: ② _____ .

CO: Could you open them, please?

N: ③ _____ .

CO: What's in this box?

N: ④ _____ .

CO: How much do you have?

N: ⑤ _____ .

CO: Have you got any cigarettes?

N: ⑥ _____ .

CO: How many are there?

N: ⑦ _____ .

CO: That's fine. You can close the suitcases now.

N: ⑧ _____ .

Role play

2 Practise the dialogue in pairs. Student A is the customs officer; B is the passenger.

Use some of the nouns from the box in Exercise 3 opposite.

A: How many/much …   do you have?
                         have you got?

B: I've got …/I have …
   Not much. Only …
   Not many. Only …
   None.

Thinking about grammar
How much … ?/How many … ?

Look at these examples:

How	many	cigarettes	are	there?
	much	snow	is	

How	many	suitcases	have you got?
	much	perfume	do you have?

3 Put these words in the table:

> water   lecturers   air   boxes   luggage
> CDs   people   food   work   men   gold
> dollars   money   carpets   sheep   kilos

How much … ?	How many … ?
perfume	suitcases
snow	cigarettes
_____	_____
_____	_____
_____	_____
_____	_____
_____	_____
_____	_____

Thinking about grammar
Possessive pronouns (*mine, yours,* etc.)

"Is this your suitcase?"

"Yes, it's mine."

Mine is a possessive pronoun. In this sentence it means 'my suitcase'. (**My** is a possessive adjective – it goes with a noun.)

4 **Underline the possessive pronouns (not possessive adjectives) in these examples.**

a) "Is this your seat?"
"No, it's yours. My seat is the next one."

b) "Are these our books on the floor?"
"No, they're his."

c) "That's her car, isn't it?"
"No, it's ours, of course!"

d) "Look, there's a handbag on that chair. Is it yours?"
"No, it belongs to that woman. It's hers."

e) "I like our house, but I think I prefer theirs. It's bigger."

5 **Complete the table.**

possessive adjective	possessive pronoun
my bag	mine
your bag	
his bag	
her bag	
our bag	
their bag	

6 **Write in the possessive pronouns:** *mine, yours, his, hers, ours, theirs.*

A — "I think it's _____."

B — "Give me that case. It's not _____! It's _____!"

C — "Whose is this passport?"
"I think it's _____."

D — "Flight BA456 to Zurich, Gate 6."
"Yes, that's _____. Let's go."

E — "They're _____, I think."
"Whose are these drinks?"

Skills in Focus – listening and speaking

Listening

1 You are going on a camping trip with family or friends. In a group, make a list of all the things you need to take.

2 Listen to Lee and Hassan and check your ideas. Write any extra items you hear.

Survey

3 Ask ten people you know: 'Choose three countries from this list that you would most like to visit: Kenya, Jamaica, China, France, Japan, Brazil, Ireland, Thailand.'

4 Make a table like this. Write in the countries.

name	1st country	2nd country	3rd country
Suzie	Japan	Brazil	Thailand

5 Use a bar chart to show your results.

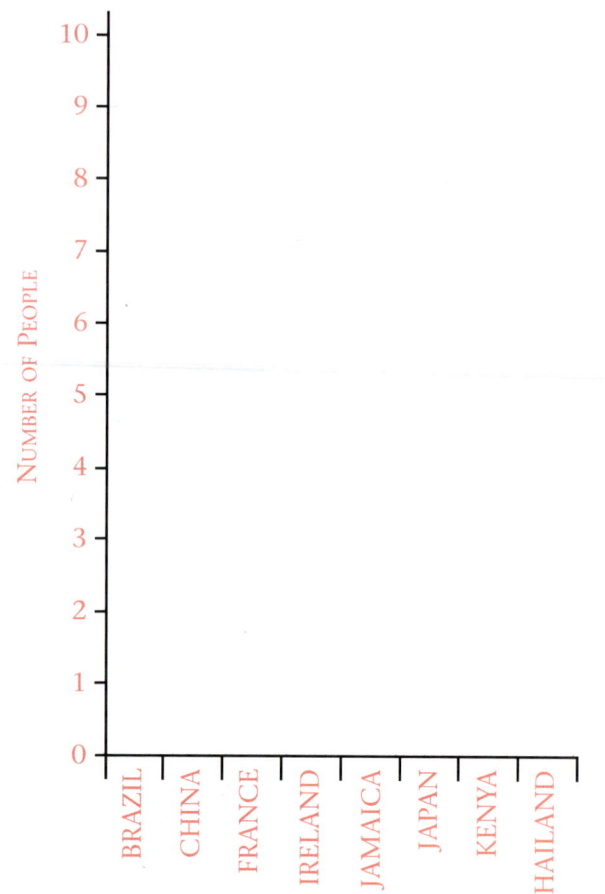

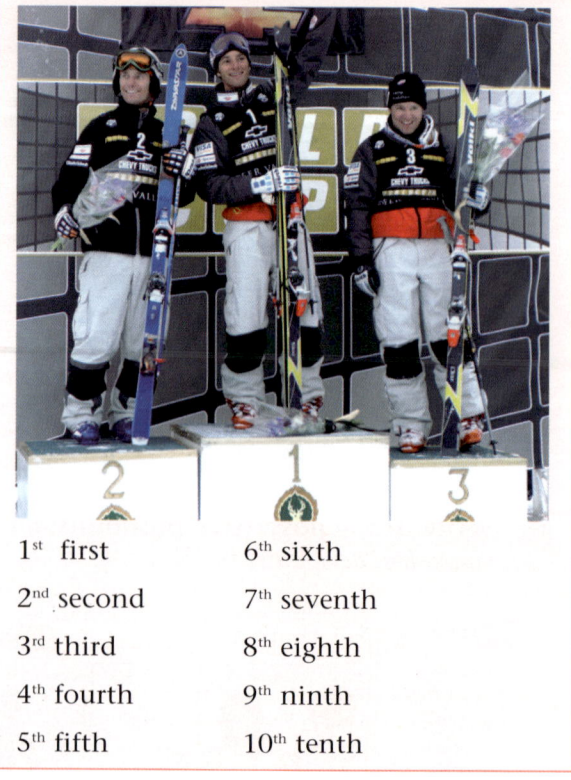

Ordinal numbers

1st	first	6th	sixth
2nd	second	7th	seventh
3rd	third	8th	eighth
4th	fourth	9th	ninth
5th	fifth	10th	tenth

6 Prepare a short talk to describe your results. Use the table and chart to help you. Use these phrases:

The chart shows that …

As you can see from the chart …

Reading

1 **Read this article about world tourism.**

a) Which country had the most tourists in 2000? How many tourists visited it?

b) Where in the list is China? How many visitors were there in 2000?

The most popular country on the planet!

Of all the countries in the world, which is the most popular with tourists? Is it the United Kingdom, with its historic castles and pretty villages? Or perhaps Kenya, with its wild animals and beautiful beaches? Maybe it is the United States, with the exciting attractions of New York and Disneyland?

The answer is none of these. The country with the most tourists is in fact France. With its beautiful scenery, pleasant climate and wonderful food and wine, France seems to be the place that everyone wants to visit. In addition, it has one of the most attractive cities in the world, Paris, as its capital.

According to figures for the year 2000, published by the World Tourism Organisation, 76 million tourists visited France, which was about 11% of the total number of international tourists.

The United States came in second place, with nearly 51 million tourists (7.3%). In third place was Spain, popular for its beaches and sunshine, and Italy was fourth. Spain had just over 48 million visitors (7%) and Italy had about 41 million (nearly 6%).

Perhaps the biggest surprise is the position of China in fifth place, with 31 million visitors, about 4.5% of the total. In fact, East Asia and the Pacific is the fastest growing region in the world for tourism. The region showed a 15% increase in tourist numbers during 2000.

2 **Complete the charts using information about world tourism from the article.**

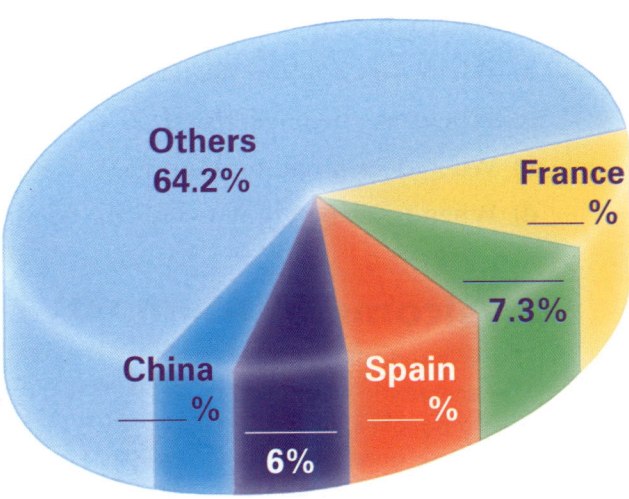

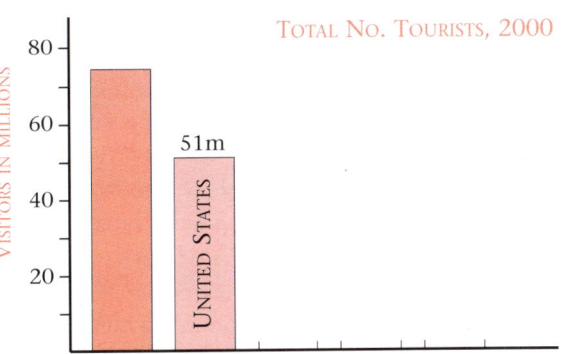

TOTAL No. TOURISTS, 2000

Adjectives

Look at the position of adjectives in these sentences:

There are many **good** hotels.

The winters are **cool** and **dry**.

There's a **small** harbour.

The capital has a **large, modern** museum.

3 **Put these words in the correct order to make sentences.**

a) many castles the in are historic Kingdom there United

b) and and France pleasant wonderful has food climate wine a

c) very the capital is attractive France of a city

Reading and writing

4 Read the description of Alumnia from a tourist guidebook.

a) Where can you find the local market?

b) Where are the hot springs?

c) When does it rain in Alumnia?

d) When is the best time to visit the country?

Welcome to Alumnia!

There is something for everyone in Alumnia. The scenery is <u>wonderful</u>: <u>high</u> mountains, lovely beaches, deserts and green valleys. There are good hotels for the visitor throughout the country, and interesting places to visit. The capital, Lobono, is a port with a population of 150,000. It has an old fort, a large, modern museum and a very colourful local market. In the picturesque harbour you can see traditional fishing boats and a fish market. Outside the city, near the new university, are famous hot springs where people swim in winter and summer. The people of Alumnia are friendly and very hospitable. They speak the local language and also French. The climate is pleasant, too. The winters are cool and dry, but very sunny. The summers are warm, with rain from time to time. September is the best month to visit because everything is green after the rains.

5 Read the description again. Underline the adjectives. Two are already underlined.

6 Write notes about Alumnia in the table.

country	Alumnia
capital	Lobono, port, population 150,000
scenery	
things to see	
people	
climate	

7 Make notes in a table about a country you know. Then write a paragraph about the country for a guidebook.

Study Tip Use your dictionary

Look at some of the information you can find in the *Longman Active Study Dictionary of English* about the word **transport**.

a) pronunciation *(phonetic transcript)*

b) part of speech *(n = noun)*

c) uncountable noun *(U = uncountable)*

d) definition *("a kind of vehicle, or … ?")*

e) example sentence *("Do you have … ?")*

f) British or American English *(BrE, AmE)*

g) related words: *transport (v)*

trans·port[1] /ˈtrænspɔːt‖-ɔːrt/ *n* [U] *BrE* **1** a kind of vehicle, or a system of buses, trains etc, that you use for going from one place to another: *Do you have your own transport?* (=do you have your own car?)|*Buses are the main form of public transport.* → see colour picture on page 669 **2** when people, goods etc are moved from one place to another; TRANSPORTATION: *the transport of live animals*

USAGE NOTE: transport

Transport is the usual British English word. The usual American English word is **transportation**. For most methods of transport, use **by** to talk about how someone gets to a place: *I came by car/plane/train* etc. However, when someone walks, use **on foot**: *I came on foot.* When you are talking about something that happens while you are using a form of public transport, use **on**: *I met Jim on the train/bus/plane* etc.

trans·port[2] /trænˈspɔːt‖-ɔːrt/ *v* [T] to move goods, people etc from one place to another in a vehicle

Reproduced by permission of Pearson Education Limited from Longman Active Study Dictionary of English, Third Edition, © Pearson Education Limited, 2000.

1 Use a dictionary to answer these questions about the word 'scenery'.

a) Give a definition of **scenery**.

b) What is wrong with this sentence: "The sceneries along the coast are wonderful!"?

c) Which is the correct pronunciation – 'skeenery' or 'seenery'?

2 Use a dictionary to complete the table. Then write four sentences using words from the table.

noun	adjective
scenery	
	hospitable
	elegant
region	

Vocabulary Review

Tourism

1 Complete the spidergram.

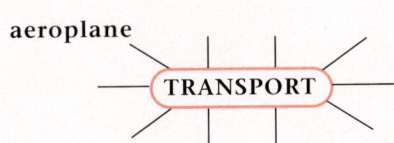

aeroplane

TRANSPORT

2 Make spidergrams for *luggage* and *tourist sights*.

Adjectives

3 Can you use these adjectives with *beaches* and *people*? Put a tick (✓) if it is possible.

	beaches	people
lovely		
friendly		
hospitable		
beautiful		
interesting		
famous		
historic		
traditional		
picturesque		

Task 1: Make a list of other new adjectives from the unit.

Task 2: Choose five adjectives from your list. Use them in sentences.

Grammar Review

- ***How much ... ?/How many ... ?***

How many	suitcases	are there?
	children	have you got?
	tickets	do you have?
How much	perfume	is there?
	money	have you got?
	food	do you have?

"**How many** children do you have?"
"Four."
"**How much** food is there in the box?"
"None."

Task 3: You are going on a picnic (or a camping trip) with a friend. Write a dialogue between the two of you. Check the list of things you are taking and the number/amount of each.

- **Position of adjectives**

Adjectives can come before nouns:

	adjective	noun
There are many	good	shops.
The town has a	small	park.

Or they can come after linking verbs (e.g., *be*, *become*):

noun	verb	adjective (complement)
The hotels	are	cheap.
The museum	is	large and modern.

They do not change their form (e.g., a **good** hotel, many **good** hotels).

- **Possessive pronouns**

possessive adjective	possessive pronoun
my bag	mine
your bag	yours
his bag	his
her bag	hers
our bag	ours
their bag	theirs

"Is this **your** bag?"
"No, it's Tariq's. It's **his**."

Introduction

Discussion

 Read these sentences about learning. Say which is true (T), not true (NT) or true in part (TP).

a) I like learning on my own. ( )

b) I like learning in a group. ( )

c) The Internet is more useful than books. ( )

d) Computers are better than teachers. ( )

2 Look at the students and the 'classrooms' in the pictures. What are the advantages and disadvantages of each situation?

Reading

3 These students are talking about how they study languages. Match the quotes with the pictures on the previous page.

A

We use computers a lot in our college. When a new student arrives, the college gives him or her a laptop computer. There are language programmes at different levels and the students follow them carefully. I like this method of learning, because students can work at their own speed.

B

We have no electricity in the school, so we don't have cassette recorders. In fact, we don't have classrooms or desks! The students sit under a tree and the teachers write on a blackboard. Studying is difficult in these conditions, especially in the rainy season! But it can also be fun.

C

I study in a large university in Spain. There are more than 200 students in our lectures. We sit in long rows. It is very difficult to learn English in such large classes. The teachers give us texts to read, and sometimes we listen to cassette recordings. We don't speak English in the class.

Listening

4 Dr Mazuki is talking about the root system of plants. Listen to the beginning of the lecture. Tick (✓) the instruction verbs you hear.

read ◯	give ◯	listen ◯
wait ◯	open ◯	do ◯
copy ◯	be ◯	make ◯
ask ◯	close ◯	stop ◯
look ◯	sit down ◯	

Classroom vocabulary

5 Label the pictures below with these words:

diagram desk table chair
blackboard equation whiteboard
chart window door wall picture
graph bookshelves

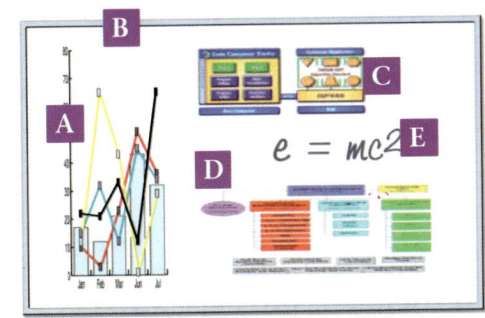

$e = mc^2$

6 What is there in your classroom? Work with a partner. Write six sentences like these:

There is a large blackboard at the front of the room.

There are some pictures on the wall.

The classroom has got two doors.

It has five rows of desks.

Language in Focus

Imperatives

1 Look at the pictures opposite. How do we make positive and negative imperatives? Complete the table.

imperative	negative imperative
Stop!	Don't stop!
Ask me.	
	Don't sit here.
	Don't copy the photo.
Listen to Pat.	

Stop!

Don't stop!

b) Write three sentences with negative imperatives for a partner. For example:

Don't smoke! It's bad for your health.

2 **a)** Look at these pictures. Complete the phrases with imperatives or negative imperatives.

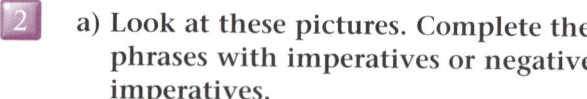

A

EMERGENCY EXIT

_____ _____ that door!

B

_____ _____ it to him!
_____ it to me!

C

_____ _____, please, and _____ talking!

_____ worry, Kim.
_____ happy!

D

NEW INTERNATIONAL UNIVERSITY

Thinking about grammar
Object pronouns (*me, you, him,* etc.)

Object pronouns take the place of object nouns in a sentence.

- Give Joe the keys. Give **him** the keys.
- Open the door, please. Open **it**, please.

3 Underline the object pronouns in these sentences.

a) Put the suitcases on the table and open them, please.

b) Shall I give you the bag?

c) Show me that book, please.

d) Please don't give us a test today.

4 Listen to two policemen (P1 and P2) and a criminal, Harry (H). Complete the dialogue with pronouns.

P1: OK. Sit down, Harry.

H: Here?

P1: Yes. Right, Harry. We want the money. Give ① _____ the money ... ***now!***

H: What? I haven't got the money.

P2: Then where is ② _____, Harry?

H: Don't ask ③ _____. Ask Joe.

P1: Joe?

H: Yeah, Joe knows. Ask ④ _____.

P2: OK. What about the diamonds? Have you got the diamonds?

H: No. I haven't got ⑤ _____.

P1: Has Joe got the diamonds, too?

H: No. Sue's got the diamonds. Ask ⑥ _____.

P2: OK, Harry, we'll give ⑦ _____ one more chance. We want the diamonds and we want the money … **now**.

H: Ask Joe and Sue. Ask ⑧ _____!

P1: OK. Joe! Sue! Come in … and meet Harry.

Direction verbs

Go	through …
Keep	going along …
Turn	right at the …
Take	the first road on your left

Match the verbs with the drawings:

a) ↱

b) ⬒⬒➡

c) ┬──┬ (dashed)

d) ➡➡➡

---

5 Read Lee's directions to the New International University student hostel and mark its location on the map with an X.

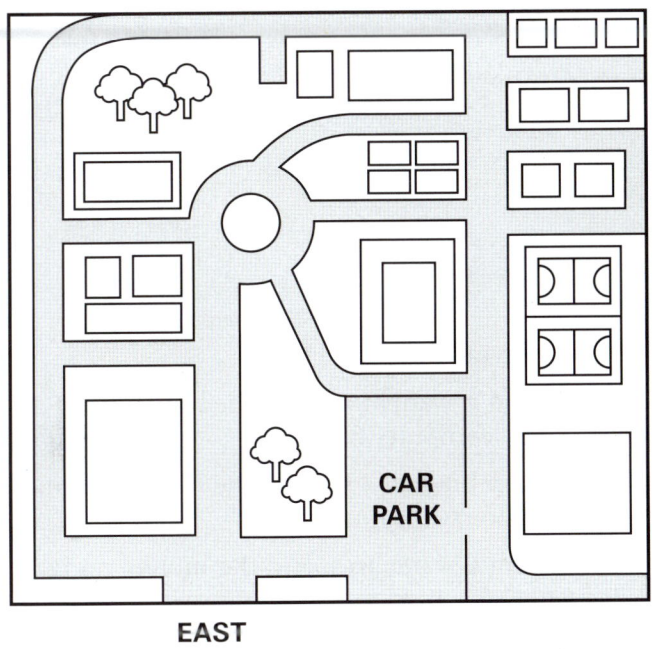

EAST GATE

Hi. Here are the directions <u>to</u> my hostel. Go <u>through</u> the East Gate of the campus and turn right. You'll see a car park <u>in front of</u> you, just next to the entrance. Go across the car park and turn left. Keep going along this road, past the basketball courts on your right and the swimming pool on the left. Take the third road on the right. The student hostel is the second building on the left. I'm on the fourth floor (don't worry, there's a lift). My room's number 34 – at the end of the corridor.

Looking forward to seeing you tomorrow at 8. Don't be late.

Lee

6 Read Lee's note again. Underline the prepositions of place and movement. Three are already underlined.

7 Complete these dialogues using the prepositions *of, across, behind, from, on, in, at, through* and *to*. You can use each preposition more than once.

a) "Where's the canteen?"

"It's _____ the right, next _____ the library."

b) "I'm looking for the lecture hall."

"It's _____ the first floor _____ the end of the corridor."

c) "Is this Mrs Khalifa's office?"

"No. Her office is _____ the next building."

"_____ the ground floor?"

"Yes, not far _____ the main entrance."

d) "Where can I find the sports hall?"

"Go _____ this park and go _____ the main door of that building – yes, the building _____ front _____ you. It's just inside."

e) "Do you know where the market is?"

"Yes. Take the first turning _____ the left. You'll see a cinema. The market is _____ the cinema."

Skills in Focus – listening and speaking

Listening

 1 Listen to a woman talking about her home. Which picture is it: A, B, C or D?

2 Listen again and answer these questions about the house.

a) What is there on the roof?

b) What is there behind the house?

c) Has the house got a balcony?

d) What is the building on the left?

e) What is the building on the right?

f) How many floors has it got?

g) What's between the house and the shop?

Debate

3 Your college/university has a problem. It has money to spend on a new computer lab, an indoor swimming pool or two new teachers, but not all three.

a) Look at the information below.

Equip your school or college for the 21st century

We are a computer hardware supplier specialising in networks for education and training. We design and set up dedicated computer-aided classrooms to your specifications – at a price you can afford.

Arrange an interview with one of our experts today.
Call 0812 397643 or e-mail us : info@netsforschools.com

b) Divide into three teams:

- **Team A** wants to spend the money on a new computer lab.

- **Team B** wants to spend the money on an indoor swimming pool.

- **Team C** wants to spend the money on two new teachers.

c) Prepare your arguments, make a list of points and choose your speakers. Debate the problem and then have a class vote.

Skills in Focus – reading and writing

Reading

1 Look at this picture of the computer lab at the New International University.

2 Read the description below and compare it with the picture of the computer lab. Work with a partner to find eight differences. Write the text out again so that it describes the picture.

THE COMPUTER LAB

There are 12 computers in the computer laboratory. There are also 12 chairs – one for each student. The computers are arranged in rows, so that there are four rows of three computers.

At the front of the room there is a desk for the Computer Studies lecturer, but there isn't a lecturer in the room at the moment. The desk is near the door, on the right. On the left of the room there is a long window, which is open. Next to the window is a chart.

Behind the desk is the whiteboard. Next to the whiteboard, on the right, is a diagram of a printer, and there are some instructions about how to print. On the left of the whiteboard there is a cupboard, and on top of the cupboard there are some books and magazines.

3 Look at the text below.

a) What is it about?

b) Why is the spelling of the title wrong?

c) Does it come from an encyclopaedia, a newspaper advertisement or a science magazine?

d) Give reasons for your answer to c).

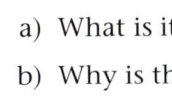

Kan yuo spel?

Do you have a problem with spelling?
Then the electronic ABC Spellchecker is for you.

What is it?

The Spellchecker has more than 150,000 words in its database. It checks and corrects words instantly. It also has a 70,000-word thesaurus, which you can use to find words that have a similar meaning. This amazing electronic machine is pocket-sized. You can take it to school or college, use it for work or for play.

How does the Spellchecker work?

It's easy to use. Just type in the word you want to check and press 'check'. The Spellchecker looks at the word and makes corrections.

It is a thesaurus.

The Spellchecker is also a thesaurus. This means that it is a kind of dictionary. It can give you words that have a similar meaning. For example, if you type in the word 'diagram', it will give you the words 'plan' and 'drawing'. This is useful for writing essays and also for word games.

What else can it do?

The ABC Spellchecker has a number of other functions.

It is a calculator.

It can calculate sums up to ten digits long. It is a currency converter. It converts quickly from one currency to another. It is ideal for holidays and business. It is a games centre. It has 10 different word games – ideal for passing the time. Take it with you on long journeys. It is a word saver. It can store up to 50 words.

Amazing!

It is truly amazing that this pocket-sized machine has so many functions. But that is not the only amazing thing. The price is just $19. Order your ABC Spellchecker today!

4 Read the text and find answers to these questions:

a) Does the Spellchecker have games?

b) What is a thesaurus?

c) Can you use the machine for calculations?

d) How big is it?

e) How much does the Spellchecker cost?

5 Look at the underlined words in the text.

a) What do you think they mean?

b) Use a dictionary to check your answers.

c) Find words with a similar meaning.

6 Look at the circled words. What kind of verbs are they? Put them in these sentences:

a) _____ two aspirins with a little water every day.

b) For instant home delivery _____ your pizzas by phone.

c) Just _____ the switch marked 'on' to start the machine.

d) Please _____ your name at the top of the page.

Writing

7 Write a paragraph about the room in the picture below or a room you know well. Use these forms:

There is/are …

on the left/on the right/at the front

behind/in front of/on top of/next to/near

8 Find out some information about a machine or instrument, for example, a mobile phone, cassette recorder or watch. Write an advertisement for a newspaper like the Spellchecker advertisement. Give details of price, features, functions, size, etc.

Study Skills and Review

Study Tip   Learn a word – and its friends!

● When you learn a word, learn its collocations (the words that go with it). For example, 'at the end of the' goes with 'corridor'. These verbs go with 'graph':

verb	a graph (noun)
to draw	✓
to write	✗
to describe	✓
to do	✗
to plot	✓
to read	✓

and 'language' collocates with these nouns:

language ⟨ practice / laboratory / programme / class

1 Complete the table with ticks and crosses to show the collocations.

	a question	a person	a picture
ask	✓	✓	✗
answer			
describe			
listen to			
draw			

2 What collocations are there with the word 'instructions'? Complete the diagram below with more verbs. Use a dictionary to help you.

to read ⟩ instructions

3 Now find six nouns that collocate with 'training'. For example: training *course*, *language* training.

4 Use the collocations you found to write four sentences using 'instructions' and 'training'.

Vocabulary Review

In the classroom

1 Complete the spidergram.

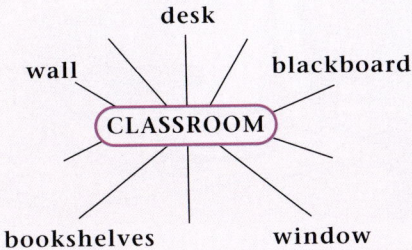

2 Make spidergrams for:
   a) Classroom instruction verbs (*read*, *wait*, *copy*, etc.)
   b) Visuals (*charts*, *graphs*, etc.)

Grammar Review

- ### Imperatives

   Don't be late.

   Wait outside the room until the examiner shows you in.

   Take everything that you need with you.

   Don't copy from your neighbour.

- ### Pronouns

possessive adjective	possessive pronoun	object pronoun
my	mine	_____
your	_____	you
his	_____	his
her	hers	_____
_____	its	it
our	ours	_____
their	_____	_____

Task 1: Complete the table.

Language Review

- ### Giving directions

   Go across/straight/through …

   Turn left/right at the crossroads.

   Keep straight on/going along.

   Take the (first) turning on the left/right.

   Task 2: Work in pairs. Give your partner directions to a place you both know (don't tell him/her what it is). Can he/she follow your directions to find the place?

Go straight ahead and take the 198th turning on the left and then the 249th turning on the right …

- ### Describing places/Describing objects

   There is/are …

   It has/has got …

   It doesn't have/hasn't got …

   It can …

REVIEW UNIT A

Listening: Part 1

 Listen to Indira's tutorial about exam revision and complete the diagram with these words:

> quiet place   brain   planned breaks
> concentrate   stationery

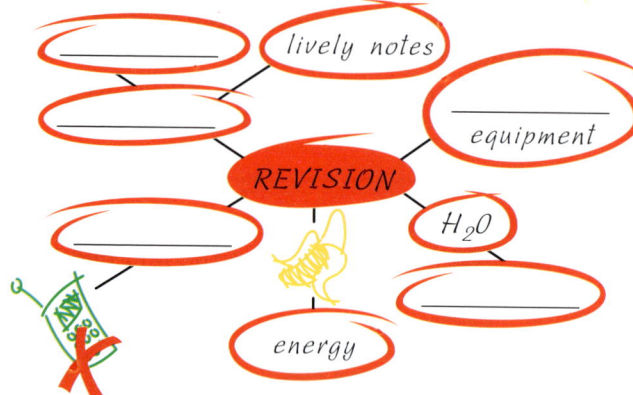

2 Try to fill in the missing words. Then listen again and check your answers.

Indira: Today we're going to look at some strategies for revision. First I'd like to hear some of your suggestions for successful revision.

Hassan: Make sure you ① _____ everything you need: books, notepaper, printer paper, disks, pencils, notes and so on.

Nina: I read this somewhere – before you sit down at ② _____ desk to start work, drink ③ _____ glass of water. ④ _____ sips regularly while you work – this ⑤ _____ you to concentrate.

Hassan: I read that, too. And eat a banana. That will raise your blood sugar levels and give ⑥ _____ energy. But ⑦ _____ have ⑧ _____ cake or biscuits – they make you sleepy.

Pedro: You need somewhere quiet …

Indira: So ⑨ _____ to switch your mobile phone off!

Pedro: Sorry about that.

Indira: Now what next? Plan to make the best possible use of your most incredible piece of equipment – your brain.

Hassan: How do we do that?

Indira: Well, there ⑩ _____ two ways you can make the most of your brain's ability to learn. Firstly, make your notes as lively, entertaining and creative as possible. Secondly, take lots of planned breaks.

Pedro: That sounds too good to be true!

Language in Focus:
Imperatives

3 Indira and the students use a lot of instruction verbs or imperatives to give advice and instructions.

a) Look back at the tapescript for Exercise 2. Find and underline all the imperatives. The first one is done as an example.

b) Give advice about exams using the following verb and phrases:

Plan _____ .

Use _____ .

Make _____ .

Take _____ .

Don't forget _____ .

Don't worry about _____ .

Don't do _____ .

Listening: Part 2

4 Write the questions below in the correct place in the tapescript. Then listen to the next part of the tutorial to check.

Nina: Is that why it's important to include colour and drawings in our note-taking?

Hassan: Are there other advantages?

Nina: Are you sure it works?

Hassan: So what's the alternative?

Nina: But aren't notes very important when you prepare for exams?

Nina: Where do our brains store mind maps?

Pedro: Er, isn't it break time now?

Hassan: How do we do that?

① _____

Indira: Yes, they are. However, don't write notes line by line – that isn't very helpful. It makes lots of A4 paper, which is time-consuming and difficult to revise from.

Pedro: So no more note-taking! Yippee!

Indira: I didn't say that!

② _____

Indira: Try note-mapping. It is active and creative. You start at the centre of a piece of paper and write your notes out from there.

③ _____

Indira: Put your main subject in the middle. Then choose the important areas that join it. One word is usually enough for one idea. Or you can use colour and simple drawings.

④ _____

Indira: Yes. It is easier to remember information in a map than written notes.

⑤ _____

Indira: There are lots. It uses less space. And as with other maps, they can show you several ways to the same place and help show you how one area joins with another. Mapped notes are very useful when you want to select information to answer an exam question.

⑥ _____

Indira: Well, in the classroom, we mostly use the left side of our brain. This controls logic, language and number. But if we also try to use the 'artistic' right side of the brain, we can store information better.

⑦ _____

Indira: Yes, exactly. No two sets of mapped notes are the same. Because they are individual, they are easy to remember – not like traditional notes. Now, I also mentioned planning your breaks …

⑧ _____

Indira: Yes, it's half past four. So I will give you a handout to study in your own time which explains about planning breaks.

Language in Focus:
Antonyms

5 On the left are some adjectives from the tapescript. Match them with their opposites on the right.

a) helpful	1) unimaginative
b) easy	2) modern
c) quick	3) unhelpful
d) active	4) useless
e) creative	5) time-consuming
f) useful	6) difficult
g) traditional	7) inactive

Language in Focus:
Pronouns and prepositions

6

Nina is visiting her friend Alia. Read their conversation and choose the correct word for each space. Then listen and check your answers.

Alia: Hi, Nina! Come ① *on/in/off*.

Nina: Hello. How are you?

Alia: Fine. How was ② *you/your/yours* tutorial?

Nina: Good. I usually hate having tutorials ③ *at/in/on* Monday morning, but this one was very interesting.

Alia: What was it about?

Nina: Well, Mrs Hussein gave ④ *our/we/us* some really useful tips about revision and note-taking. It made ⑤ *me/my/I* think about how I organise ⑥ *me/my/I* notes.

Alia: Sounds good. Did ⑦ *your/you/yours* take any notes, then?

Nina: Of course ⑧ *me/my/I* did!

Alia: Wow! ⑨ *Their/They/Them* are covered in pictures! Your notes are really colourful. ⑩ *Mine/My/Me* are always so boring I fall asleep when I read ⑪ *they/their/them*!

Nina: That's probably because you revise ⑫ *at/in/on* night and you never take any breaks …

Reading and study skills

7

a) Read section 1 of Indira's handout *Reviewing Your Work* and complete the note map.

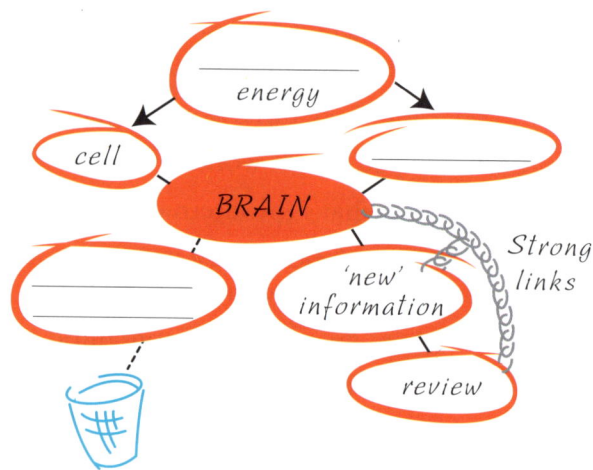

b) Read section 2 and complete the note map.

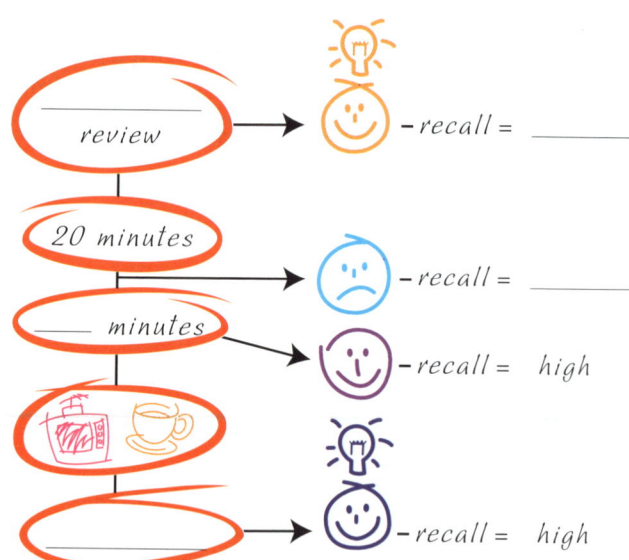

c) Read section 3 and choose the best question for a heading from this list:

How do I review my work?

Where do I review my work?

Are reviews effective?

Reviewing Your Work

1 Why is it important to review information?
Brain activity is chemical energy travelling between brain **cells**. The brain is **continuously** finding information, so it is making new links all the time. But this means it 'forgets' some old links. That's why it is important to review information we want to remember.

Study tip!
The more you revise, the stronger the **neural** links become and the more quickly you can remember.

2 Why plan breaks?
The timing of reviews is important, and this is why you need to plan your breaks. Don't lock yourself away for a long time. This is unhelpful, because the brain's ability to **recall** is better at the start and finish of periods of learning. After 20–50 minutes of studying, your ability to remember facts quickly begins to **decline**

Study tip!
A ten-minute break and then a short self-test is an **effective** way to **consolidate** what you have just studied.

3
_____

_____

The most effective way is to take three **approaches**:

VISUAL
Make your notes colourful and pictorial and they will have visual **appeal**. Use them as wall displays or put them on cards.

AUDITORY
Talk yourself through your notes or explain them to others – parents, friends or maybe the cat! You will quickly see where your understanding is good … and where it is not.

KINAESTHETIC
Add movement of some sort. For example, try putting dates or formulas on the floor and walking from one to the next as you review your ideas. Crazy? Maybe. But you have a **set** of physical **associations** to help you remember what you know more accurately.

Study tip!
For more ideas visit www.learn.co.uk

Inferring meanings of new words

8 Read the handout again and write one of the blue words next to each definition.

a) Remember. _____

b) To make something stronger. _____

c) Relating to the body's system of nerves. _____

d) Without stopping. _____

e) Become weaker, less powerful. _____

f) A group or collection. _____

g) Attraction or interest _____

h) The smallest parts of an animal or plant that can live independently. _____

i) Connections. _____

j) Relating to things you can see. _____

k) Working well, successful. _____

l) Ways of completing a task. _____

m) Relating to things you can hear. _____

Introduction

Discussion

1 **Look at these pictures of cities from around the world. Work in groups.**

a) Try to name the cities.

b) Choose two of the cities. Say what you know about them.

c) Now compare the two cities. What is the same and what is different about them?

Reading

2 Read about this capital city – X. Which city is it?

This capital city has a population of ten million. X is not on the coast. It is located on a river, hundreds of miles from the sea. The river has the same name as the city.

The winters are very cold – colder than in London or Tokyo, and also very long. There is usually a lot of snow. The summer, however, is better than the winter. It is warm and sometimes very hot. Spring and autumn are both rather short seasons, shorter than summer or winter.

The city is older than Tokyo, but not as old as London. It was founded in the 12th century. It has many beautiful buildings and more museums and art galleries than any city I know. In the centre is a very large and famous fort, called the Kremlin.

Listening

3 Shaheen, an Indian student at the NIU, is giving a talk about Mumbai and Delhi. Listen and complete the table.

	Delhi	Mumbai
population	8 million	
location		in the west, on the coast
climate		hot and humid, rain in the summer
founded	12th century	
economy		financial centre, port, textiles, film industry

4 Decide if these sentences are true or false. Correct the false statements.

a) Mumbai's population is greater than Delhi's.

b) Delhi is older than Mumbai.

c) Delhi's climate is wetter than Mumbai's.

d) Mumbai is more industrial than Delhi.

Vocabulary

5 Match the adjectives with their opposites.

long · new · hot · beautiful · short · bad · good · ugly · wet · expensive · cheap · old · tall · small · light · short · big · cold · heavy · dry

6 Match the pictures with the following words: airport, motorway, bus station, museum, fort, street, hospital, road, market, railway station, roundabout, office block, hotel.

7 Make two lists from the words above, under the headings *buildings* and *roads*. Add any other words you know to the lists.

Language in Focus

Thinking about grammar
Comparing

a) Mumbai is **big**.
Mumbai is **bigger** than Delhi.

b) Delhi is **old**.
Delhi is **older** than Mumbai.

c) Mumbai is **wet**.
Mumbai is **wetter** than Delhi.

Spelling

- Most adjectives are regular.

    cold – cold**er**   short – short**er**

    small – small**er**   great – great**er**

- Some adjectives have a double consonant.

    big – bi**gg**er   hot – ho**tt**er

    wet – we**tt**er

- Adjectives ending in 'y' change 'y' for 'i':

    dry – dr**ier**   heavy – heav**ier**

Irregular adjectives

A few adjectives are irregular.

a) Rio's climate is **good**.
Rio's climate is **better** than Brasilia's.

b) The economic situation is **bad**.
It is **worse** than last year.

c) **Many** people live in Lahore.
More people live in Karachi than in Lahore.

 1 Look at these encyclopaedia entries about two Spanish cities. Complete the sentences below.

Madrid Central Spain

Pop: 3 million.
Climate: Hot, dry summers.
Cool winters.
History: Founded in the 10th century, Madrid became the capital of Spain in 1561.

Barcelona NE Spain

Pop: 1.6 million.
Climate: Hot, humid summers. Warm, wet winters.
History: Founded in 230 BC, Barcelona is the second largest city in Spain.

a) Madrid has a (big) _____
population _____ Barcelona.

b) Barcelona has (warm) _____ winters
_____ Madrid.

c) Madrid is (dry) _____ _____
Barcelona in summer.

d) Barcelona is (old) _____ _____
Madrid.

2 Now write sentences about Beirut and Cairo using the information below.

Beirut Lebanon

Pop: 1.5 million.
Climate: Hot, humid summers. Warm, wet winters.
History: Founded in 1,500 BC, Beirut became the capital of the

Cairo N Egypt

Pop: 7 million.
Climate: Hot, dry summers. Cool, dry winters.
History: Founded in AD 641, Cairo is the largest city in Africa.

Thinking about grammar

Question forms – *have/has got*

3 Underline the question forms in these examples.

a) It has got a bus station.
Has it got an airport?

b) You have got a son.
Have you got any daughters?

c) Rosa has got a sister.
Has she got any brothers?

d) They have got a boat.
Have they got a car?

4 Complete the short answers to Exercise 3.

a) Yes, it _____.

b) No, I _____.

c) No, she _____.

d) Yes, _____ _____.

Question forms – *do/does*

5 Match sentences from A and B to make short dialogues. Underline the **do/does** question forms, as in the example.

A Lobono has many parks.

Most people here speak French.

<u>Do we have</u> an exam in this subject?

Are you OK, Sarah?

Do you live in Ankara?

Tony is very rich.

B Yes, we do. We have a house in the suburbs.

Oh? Does he work in a bank?

Yes, of course. Do I look ill?

Does it have a market?

Do they understand English, too?

Yes, at the end of the semester.

6 Complete the table.

Do you (we/they) … ?	Yes, I _____.
	No, I _____.
Does he (she/it) … ?	Yes, he _____.
	No, _____ doesn't.

7 You are a new student at the NIU. Make questions about the university using *have/has got*.

a) university/good sports facilities?

b) libraries/Internet connections?

c) hostels/kitchens?

d) administration building/a lift?

e) Engineering Faculty/canteen?

8 Put the words in order to make 'yes/no' questions.

a) job/got/Julia/new/a/has ?

b) any/you/do/have/children ?

c) at/Rosa/NIU/study/the/does ?

d) Spanish/speak/they/Brazil/do/in ?

e) luggage/a/have/of/got/you/lot ?

f) hat/I/look/this/stupid/in/do ?

Asking for information

9 Nadia is talking to Suzanne about her hometown. Put these questions in the right places in the dialogue, then listen and check.

> **Has it got an airport?**
> **What's the population?**
> **Does it have hot summers?**
> **What are the main attractions?**
> **Is that in Egypt?** **What's it like?**
> **Are there many old buildings?**

S: Where are you from, Nadia?

N: I'm from Aswan.

S: Aswan? ① _____

N: Yes, that's right. In the south.

S: ② _____

N: It's a small city. It's very beautiful. It's on the River Nile.

S: It sounds nice. ③ _____

N: About a quarter of a million.

S: That's quite big. ④ _____

N: Yes, it does. Very hot. But the winters are much cooler.

S: ⑤ _____

N: Yes, of course. It's an ancient city.

S: Really? ⑥ _____

N: Yes. There's a big one. We have a lot of tourists, you see.

S: ⑦ _____

N: The Aswan High Dam and Abu Simbel Temples.

S: It sounds great!

Skills in Focus – listening and speaking

Speaking

1 Work with a partner. Compare these planets, buildings and airports.

For example:

Mars has more satellites than Earth.
JFK Airport is bigger than Heathrow.

Name	**Earth**
Diameter	**12,756 km**
No. of satellites	**1 (the moon)**
Distance from the sun	**150 million km**
Average temperature	**+14°C**
Oxygen in atmosphere	**21%**

Name	**Mars**
Diameter	**6,794 km**
No. of satellites	**2**
Distance from the sun	**230 million km**
Average temperature	**-55°C**
Oxygen in atmosphere	**0.15%**

Name	**Moscow State University**	**Bank of China tower**
Built	**1940s**	**1980s**
Height	**235.7m**	**369m**
No. of floors	**36**	**72**

name	Heathrow Airport	JFK Airport
opened	1946	1948
passengers	64 million	31 million
airlines	90	125
terminals	4	9
area	1,200 hectares	2,000 hectares

2 Choose one of the pictures. Give a short talk to the class using the information.

Listening

3 Lee is talking to Rosa about his hometown in China. Listen to their conversation and make notes under the headings below.

Population   Location   Climate   Economy

4 Now listen to the conversation again. Decide if the city has the following. Put a tick (✓) or a cross (✗).

airport   ○

hospitals   ○

university   ○

railway station   ○

market   ○

hotels   ○

Speaking

5 Work in a small group.

a) Choose a world city for the next Olympic Games. Why would your city be a good place for the games? Discuss the location, the climate, the size of the city, distance from other countries, etc.

b) Now give a talk to the class. Explain the reasons for your choice.

Skills in Focus – reading and writing

Reading

1 Look at the picture of Hong Kong on page 50. What do you know about Hong Kong and its airport? Discuss in small groups.

2 Read about Hong Kong's new airport.

a) What is the name of the airport?

b) What was Hong Kong's problem?

c) What was the solution to the problem?

d) How far is the new airport from the city?

e) How can people get from the airport to the city?

f) What is special about the airport terminal?

AN AIRPORT IN THE SEA

Hong Kong is a prosperous city, situated on the southeast coast of China. It is an important financial and business centre with a growing population. But a few years ago Hong Kong had a problem. The airport, at Kai Tak near the city centre, was too small for the increasing number of passengers. Hong Kong needed a new, bigger, better airport.

Hong Kong, however, is very small. It is surrounded by mountains on one side and the South China Sea on the other, and so there is very little flat land for building airports. The answer to the problem was quite simple. They decided to build an airport in the sea.

Near Hong Kong is a small island called Chek Lap Kok. The island was flattened and made four times bigger. The airport buildings and the runways were built on this island and a bridge was built to connect the island to the mainland.

Chek Lap Kok Airport, located about 40 kilometres from the city centre, was opened in 1998 by the Chinese President, Jiang Zemin. It is a beautiful airport in an amazing location. It took six years to build. The cost was enormous – more than $20 billion. The bridge has a main span of 1.4 kilometres and carries a railway and a motorway.

The airport is much larger than the old Kai Tak Airport and has a greater capacity. It can handle 80 million passengers a year. The terminal building is the largest covered space in the world. There are more than 100 shops and restaurants and it is 1.5 kilometres long.

As cities become larger and a greater number of people want to fly, more and more airports will be built in the sea. Where cities do not have sufficient flat land, it could be the answer to the problem.

New airport at Chek Lap Kok

Existing airport at Kai Tak

Kowloon

Lantau Island

Hong Kong Island

Lamma Island

——— Road Link
——— Rail Link
≍ New Bridge

Writing

3 Write a paragraph about one of the three cities below or a city you know. Use the information in the table or find out information about your city.

	Bangkok	Rio de Janeiro	Sydney
country	Thailand (capital)	Brazil	Australia
population	6.6 million	6 million	4 million
location	southwest Thailand, divided in two by Chao Phraya River	southeast Brazil, on Atlantic, beautiful location	southeast Australia, on Pacific, large natural harbour, beautiful beaches
climate	Very hot, humid summers. Rain May–October	hot summers & warm winters	warm winters, mild, wet winters
founded	18th century, by Chakri dynasty	18th century, by Portuguese	18th century, by British
economy	commercial, tourist & finance centre	manufacturing centre, port, tourist centre	port, commercial & economic centre, tourist centre

4 Write a letter to the Olympic Committee proposing the city you chose for the next Olympic Games. Give reasons for your choice.

Dear Sirs,

I would like to suggest that you choose Rio de Janeiro as the location for the next Olympic Games.

As you probably know, Rio is a beautiful city …

I know that the games are held in July and August. These are winter months in Rio and the weather is very …

There are also many sports stadiums in Rio, which can …

Finally, Brazilians love sport. I am sure they will want …

I hope you will consider my suggestion.

Yours faithfully

Study Skills and Review

Study Tip If you don't know a word … guess!

If we look up every new word in a dictionary it makes reading very slow. We can often guess the meaning of a word by:

- **Using the context** – the other words around the unknown word – to help us get the meaning, e.g.:

  a) The city is very **prosperous**. It has many banks and businesses.

  b) It was **founded** in the 7th century.

  c) 'Has it got any old buildings?' 'Yes, of course. It's an **ancient** city.'

  We can guess that the meanings are:

  a) rich   b) built   c) very old

- **Using the form** of the word, e.g.:

  a) The island was **flattened** and made four times its size.

  b) Some of the new buildings are very **unattractive**.

  c) My French is quite good, but sometimes I **misunderstand** when people speak quickly.

  If we know the word 'flat', we can guess the meaning of the verb *flattened* in a). If we know that *un-* or *mis-* at the beginning of a word mean 'opposite', then we can guess the meanings of *unattractive* and *misunderstand*.

1 Try to guess the meaning of these words from the context.

a) Winters in Moscow can be *bitterly* cold. Temperatures often drop to –20 °C.

b) The old airport in Hong Kong had only one *runway*. Planes landing on the runway had to pass close to tall buildings.

c) A suspension bridge across the river is nearly one kilometre long. The main *span* is 500 metres.

d) The cost of the project was *enormous* – more than $20 billion.

2 Guess the meaning of these words from the word form.

a) They plan to **modernise** the hospital.

b) The water is **undrinkable**.

c) We have a **dehumidifier** in the apartment.

d) There may be **climatic** changes in the future.

e) The weather is **unseasonable** at the moment.

Vocabulary Review
Places

1 Put these words in order, starting with the smallest: *city, town, continent, district, province, village, country.*

village

2 Make spidergrams for:

a) buildings

b) roads

Weather

3 Complete the tables of weather vocabulary with adjectives and nouns.

noun	adjective	noun	adjective
heat	hot	snow	
	humid		dry
sun		wind	
rain			cold

What other weather/climate words do you know?

Grammar Review

• Comparing

Task 1: Complete the table.

adj.	comparative	adj.	comparative
big great	bigger greater	small	smaller
long tall	longer taller	short	shorter
cold	colder	hot	hotter
wet	_____	dry	_____
old	_____	new	_____
		young	_____
heavy	_____	light	_____
good	_____	bad	_____

Task 2: Write five true sentences using comparatives from your table.

For example:

Ankara is colder than Istanbul in winter.
Singapore has a much smaller population than Malaysia.
Hong Kong's new airport is much bigger than the old one.

• Question forms

Present simple

Do	I/we you/they	need know	to take notes? the way?
Does	he/she it	live have	in Lobono? an airport?

have/has got

Have	I/we you/they		time? a car?
Has	he/she it	got	children? an airport?

Language Review

• Asking for information

What's it like?

Is there/Are there … ?

Has it got … ?

Does it have … ?

• Giving information

It's (beautiful/old/big).

There is/are …

It's got …

It has …

Introduction

Discussion

1 Look at the pictures. Discuss the questions in groups.

a) Where is this instrument from?

b) What is it used for?

c) Where is this stone circle?

d) Is it natural or man-made?

e) What do you think the stones were for?

f) What is a computer used for?

g) Computers help machines to walk and talk, but can computers think? Are they intelligent?

Computer vocabulary

2   Work with a partner. Find ten 'computer words' below and use them to label the pictures.

(disk)   mirror   arrow   mouse   jacket
screen   monitor   rat   file   printer
orange   keyboard   menu   road
speakers   engine

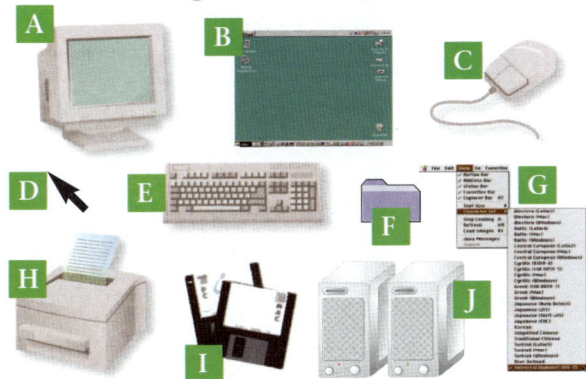

3   Match the computing 'instruction verbs' with the pictures: *click, drag, point, open, close, copy, cut, paste, print.*

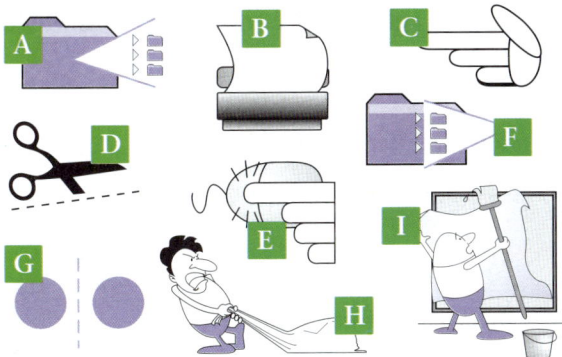

4   What other computer verbs and nouns do you know? Work with a partner and make a list.

Listening

5   Fatima and Pat are in the computer lab at the New International University. What problem does Fatima have with her computer?

6   Listen to Fatima and Pat again. Number these instructions 1 to 6.

Move the arrow down the list.	◯	Point the arrow at 'File'.	◯
Click on 'File'.	◯	Click on 'OK'.	◯
Select 'All'.	◯	Click on 'Print'.	◯

Reading

7   Read this article about computers and complete it with the words from the box.

equipment   watches   machine   program
pictures   computer   bar codes
instructions   jobs   calculations

COMPUTERS

What is a computer? A computer is a

① _____ that can do a number of different

tasks or ② _____. It makes very quick

③ _____. It reads information. It can also

produce sounds and ④ _____.

Can a computer think? A computer is not

really very intelligent. It is very fast and it

stores large amounts of data, but a computer

can't think. It needs a ⑤ _____

to tell it what to do.

How does a computer program work?

A computer program is just a long list of

simple ⑥ _____. They are stored

inside the computer. The computer reads the

instructions and then follows them one

by one.

Where do we use computers? Computers

are everywhere. Shopkeepers use them to

read ⑦ _____ and rocket scientists

use them to guide satellites. Sometimes we

don't know that we are using a ⑧ _____.

For example, there are very small computers

in electronic ⑨ _____ like video

recorders, mobile phones and ⑩ _____.

Language in Focus

Thinking about grammar
'Wh-' questions

1 Look at these question words from the article on page 59.

- **What** is a computer?
- **How** does a computer program work?
- **Where** do we use computers?

2 What other 'wh-' question words are there? Complete the table.

wh-	aux.	subject	verb
What			work?
Where	do	I/you/we/they	use?
How			open?
_____			close?
_____	does	he/she/it	put?
_____			want?
_____			like?

3 Put the words in order to make 'wh-' questions.

a) you/do/live/where ?

b) close/we/file/how/the/do ?

c) bar codes/shopkeepers/use/why/do ?

d) the/close/does/supermarket/when ?

4 Match your questions with these answers.

- Nine thirty, I think.
- So that they can keep a record of their goods.
- Near the station.
- First click on 'File'.

Asking for and giving help

5 Look at the computer screens. Now listen to Mark and the teacher.

a) Mark wants a document. What is the name of the document?

b) Number the pictures 1, 2 and 3.

6 Listen again and complete the conversation.

T: Hello, Mark. ① _____?

M: Yes, please, Mr Perez. ② _____ open a document?

T: Have you worked on it recently?

M: Yes, this morning.

T: Then it's easy. ③ _____ on 'Start'.

M: ④ _____?

T: There ... at the bottom of the screen.

M: Right. ⑤ _____?

T: Now move the arrow up the menu and ⑥ _____ 'Documents'.

M: Yes, I see. 'Documents'.

T: ⑦ _____ do you want?

M: Er ... that one. 'First-Year Maths'.

T: Right. Now click on 'First-Year Maths'.

M: That's it! Thanks very much.

Thinking about grammar
how and which

 Look at these examples.

- How do I open a document?
- How can I print a file?

Is there a difference in the meanings of 'How do I ...' and 'How can I ...'?

Now look at these examples.

- Which document do you want?
- Which do you prefer – listening to the radio or watching TV?

Is which used in the same way in the two examples?

 Complete these questions with *how* or *which*.

a) _____ do I phone Indonesia?

b) _____ is my cup – this one or that one?

c) _____ can I get to the library from here?

d) _____ floor is the canteen on – the ground floor or the first floor?

e) _____ do you switch on the printer?

f) _____ computer have you got?

 Match the questions above with these answers.

> Go along the corridor and turn right.

> The first, I think.

> Actually, I don't have one.

> The blue one with the white handle.

> Press the red button.

> Do you know the code?

Subject and object questions

10 **What is the difference between these two examples?**

a) 'Who likes modern art?'
   'Jamie likes modern art.'

b) 'Who do you like best – Picasso or Van Gogh?'
   'I like Van Gogh best.'

In one example who is the subject – in the other, who is the object. Which is which?

11 **Complete these questions with *Who* or *What*.**

a) '_____ plays football?' 'Sam and Joe.'

b) '_____ does Toni play?' 'Cricket.'

c) '_____ likes Madonna?' 'Mary.'

d) '_____ does Sue like?' 'Tom.'

e) '_____ eats a lot of ice-cream?' 'My brother.'

f) '_____ does Hari eat?' 'Anything!'

12 **Write questions with *Who* or *What* for these answers.**

a) Nadia watches a lot of TV.

b) Max studies Engineering.

c) Simon lives in Singapore.

d) A computer makes life easy.

e) Boris paints pictures of animals.

Skills in Focus – listening and speaking

Role play

1 Find a partner. Practise the dialogue between Mark and the teacher from page 60.

2 Practise asking for and giving help with your partner.

Student A: You are a second-year student at the New International University. Offer to help a new student. Use the language below.

Student B: You are a new student at the New International University. Ask your partner for help. Use the language below.

A: Hi. Can I help?

B: Yes. How do I   get a library card?

close a file?

save a document?

phone Mexico?

open a bank account?

check my spelling?

A: It's easy. First …

Then/Now …

B: I see./Right./Thanks.

Listening and note-taking

This is the studio of Campus Radio, a radio station run by the students of New International University. Sarah is talking to some students about three ways of communicating: *e-mails, letters* and *the telephone.*

3 Listen to the discussion and write down which of the ways of communicating each student prefers.

4 Listen again and make notes about each student.

5 a) Choose one of the three students. Write four sentences about him or her from your notes. Do not write his or her name.

b) Give your sentences to another student. Let him/her guess which student it is.

Class survey

6 Carry out a class survey. Find out which students in the class prefer to use e-mails, letters or the telephone. Write the results in the table below. Calculate the percentages.

	e-mails	letters	telephone
no. of students			
percentage of total			

Skills in Focus – reading and writing

Reading for information

1 **Discuss in groups.**

a) What does 'ordinary' mean? Give examples of: an ordinary day, an ordinary car, an ordinary town.

b) What does the 'e' in e-mail mean? Why do you think people like e-mail?

c) Put ticks (✓) or crosses (✗) in the boxes.

	fast	cheap
e-mail	○	○
telephone	○	○
ordinary mail	○	○

2 **Read the article about e-mail below. Find three things you need before you can send an e-mail message.**

E-mail – or snail mail?

You live in Bangkok but you want to send messages to a friend who is studying in New York. What do you do? Do you phone and then get very high telephone bills (and maybe wake your friend up in the middle of the night)? Or do you send letters and wait for weeks and weeks to get a reply? The first way is fast but expensive. The second (sometimes called 'snail mail') is cheap but slow. What if there was a third way that was both fast and cheap? Well, there is. It is called e-mail, and it will change your life.

What exactly is e-mail?

E-mail (electronic mail) is a way of sending messages from one computer to another. The message you type on your computer will probably appear on the screen of your friend in New York in minutes. The message can be ordinary writing, or you can attach pictures (graphics), photographs and even sounds.

What do I need?

You need three things. First, of course, you need a computer with a modem. Secondly, you need an e-mail application (such as Netscape Messenger), and thirdly, you need to know the address of the person you are writing to. An e-mail address is written on one line. It looks like this: colleges@gto.net.om. We read the address in this way: "colleges at gto dot net dot om". (We read abbreviations like 'gto' letter by letter. We read words like 'colleges' and 'net' in full.)

How do I send e-mail messages?

From the menu of your e-mail application select 'New Message'. Then type in the address of the person you are sending the message to and the subject of the message. Finally, type your message, point the arrow to the 'Send' icon and click. If you want to reply to a message, just click on the 'Reply' icon.

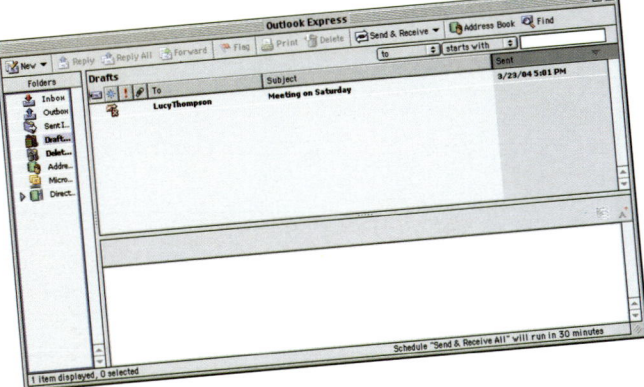

How will e-mail change my life?

You will find it much easier to keep in touch with friends and family with e-mail. There is no need for long messages, just a couple of lines to say what you want to say: 'Hello!', 'Congratulations!', 'Happy Holidays!' You can send a message anywhere in the world at any time of day – and you don't have to worry about waking people up!

3 Read the article about e-mail again. Then look at the boxes you ticked in Exercise 1 – do you want to change anything?

4 Discuss these questions with a partner.

a) What is 'snail mail'? Why is it called that?

b) What are 'graphics'? Can you send them by e-mail?

c) How do you send your message when it is ready?

d) How can you reply to a message?

Writing

5 Work in pairs. Write three real or imaginary e-mail addresses. Read them aloud to your partner. He or she must write them down.

6 Write short messages to three people in your class. Reply to the messages you receive.

7 Look at the results of your survey on page 62. In pairs, write a paragraph about the results.

Study Skills and Review

Study Tip | Ask questions!

- A good student asks lots of questions. If something is not clear, don't sit in silence. Ask the teacher or a friend. Some useful questions are:

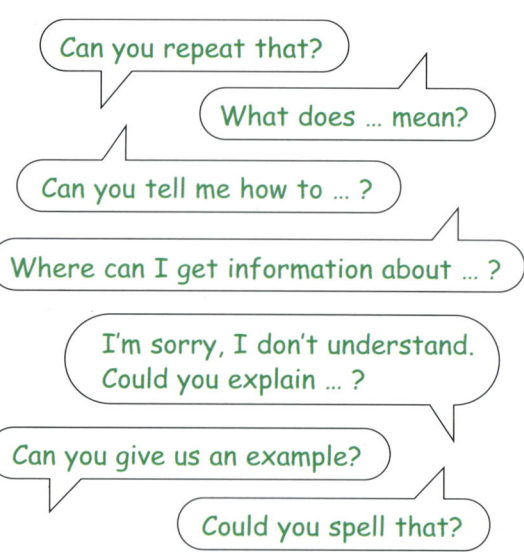

Can you repeat that?

What does ... mean?

Can you tell me how to ... ?

Where can I get information about ... ?

I'm sorry, I don't understand. Could you explain ... ?

Can you give us an example?

Could you spell that?

1 Your teacher will talk to you about uses of computers. Ask questions during the talk and at the end, and complete these notes.

Uses of computers

Six main uses:-

a) *In _____. Computers read the _____ on products.*

b) *In the _____. There are v. small computers in most _____ appliances.*

c) *In _____. Control _____.*

d) *In _____. Used to _____ students.*

e) *In scientific _____. To solve _____ and to display _____.*

f) *In _____. _____ used to do repetitive or dangerous jobs.*

Vocabulary Review

Collocations

1 Which nouns collocate with *computer*? Continue the list below.

computer   disk

screen

printer

mouse

_____

_____

_____

_____

Computing verbs

2 Draw a picture by each of these computer instruction verbs. Add other verbs you know.

click   cut

drag   select

point   move

copy   delete

Grammar Review

● Present simple – 'wh-' questions

wh-	do/does	subject	verb
When	do	I/you/we/they	work?
How			
Where	does	he/she/it	
Why			

● Subject and object questions

subject	verb	object
Who	knows	Jim? (I know Jim.)
What	annoys	Jim? (**Walkmen** annoy Jim.)

object	do/does	subject	verb
Who	does	Jim	know? (He knows **a lot of people**.)
What	does	Jim	enjoy? (Jim enjoys **music concerts**.)

● *Which*

Which do you prefer?

Which car do you prefer?

Task 1: Write seven 'wh-' questions using all of the question words.

Language Review

Offering help	Asking for help
Can I help you?	Can you help me, please?
What's the problem?	
What's the matter?	I've got a problem.
Shall I … ?	How do I … ?

Task 2: Write a dialogue between a new student and a computer instructor. Use the phrases above.

● Asking questions

Can you repeat/spell that?

What does … mean?

Could you tell me how to … ?

Where can I get information about … ?

I'm sorry, I don't understand.

Could you explain … ?

Can you give me an example?

Introduction

Discussion

1 Look at the picture of an office.

a) Find these items (A–J) in the picture: *fax machine, paperclip, computer, telephone, photocopier, printer, filing cabinet, notice board, notepad, stapler.*

b) How important are the items for a modern office? Put them in order (1 for the most important).

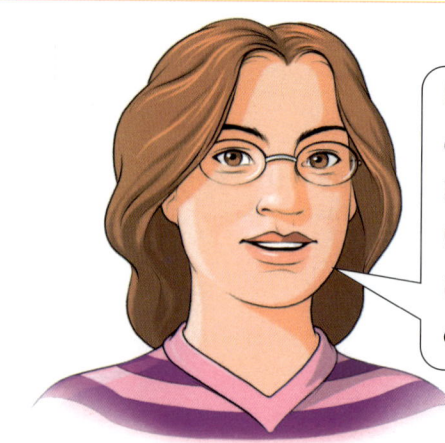

Hi, I'm Maria. I'm a secretary at the New International University. I work in the President's office.

1 ________ 2 ________ 3 ________ 4 ________ 5 ________

6 ________ 7 ________ 8 ________ 9 ________ 10 ________

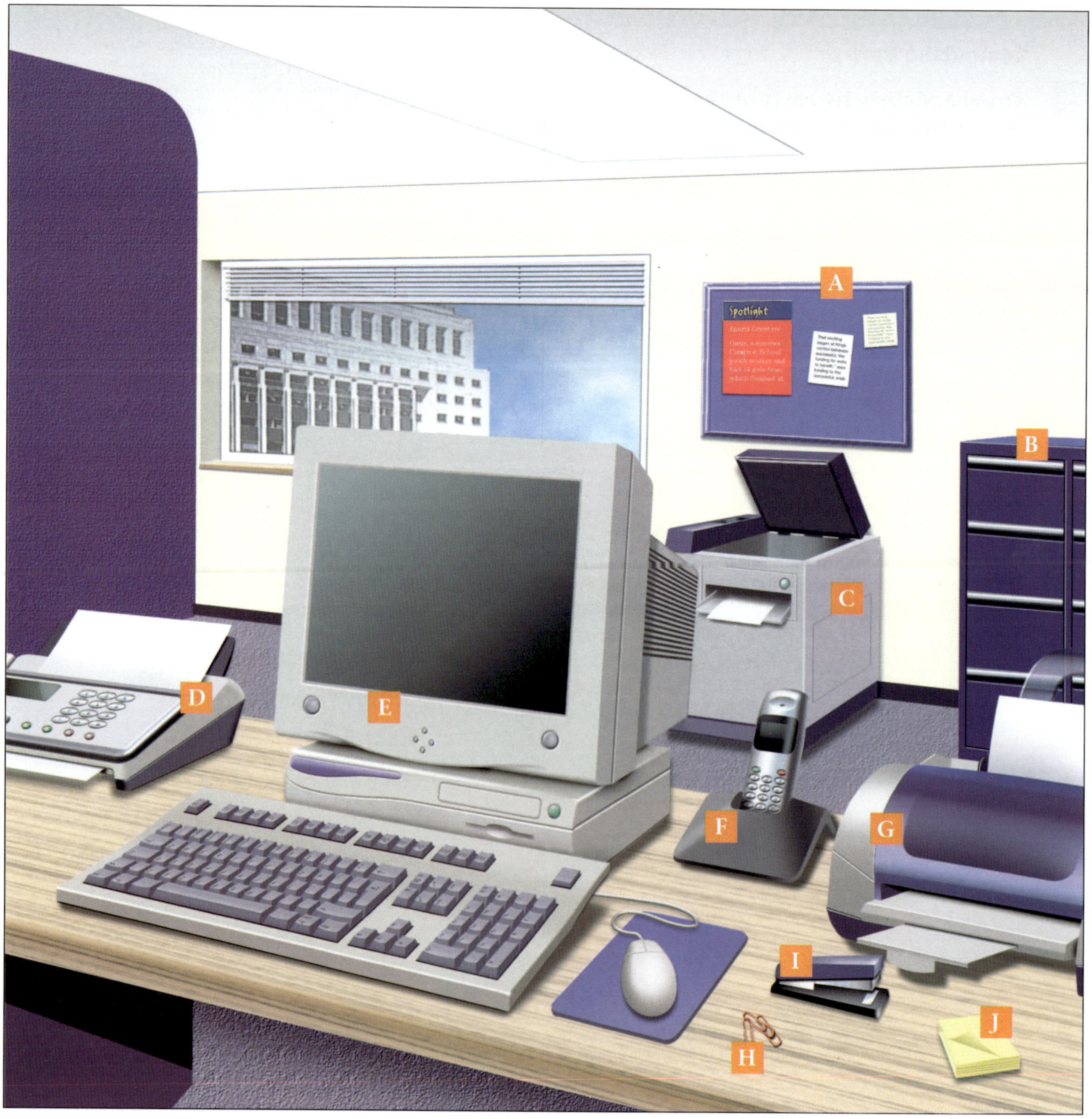
A
B
C
D
E
F
G
H
I
J
Spotlight

Listening

2 Maria is explaining how to photocopy a letter to a new secretary. Listen and put these instructions in order (1–7).

Select the number of copies you want. ◯

Wait for a few minutes. ◯

Switch off the machine. ◯

Take the letter and the photocopies from the machine. ◯

Switch on the machine. ◯

Press the start button. ◯

Put the letter on the glass. ◯

Reading

3 **Read about four people. What are their jobs?**

My name's Miriam Abbas. I work for a large electronics company called NBW Electronics in Dubai. I am a secretary in the Sales Department. I've only been here for six months. Before that I was a student at a business college in Dubai.

The job was very hard at first, because everything was new for me. But now I like it very much. I start work at eight o'clock in the morning and I finish at three in the afternoon. I don't work on Thursdays or Fridays, and so I have plenty of free time. Most of the time I have to answer the telephone and speak to visitors to the company. I also write letters on the computer and send faxes.

Last year, Kim was a student at a college of journalism. Now he is a sports writer on one of Hong Kong's best newspapers – the *Daily Record*. He is very lucky, because he loves sport and he loves writing.

His job is to go to sports events in Hong Kong, such as football matches and horse races, and write about them. He also has to interview people. Kim doesn't travel to other countries – he only writes about sport in Hong Kong. He usually starts work at ten o'clock and finishes about seven o'clock in the evening. Sometimes, however, he has to work very late.

Hector and Julio are brothers. They live in Rio de Janeiro in Brazil. Two years ago they were students at university. Now they are tour guides. They work in their father's travel company – Tropical Travel.

Their duties are to plan tours for foreign visitors, meet tourists at the airport and take them to their hotels. They both speak French and English, as well as Portuguese. Julio also speaks German.

They don't like the work very much. They have to start work very early in the morning – at six o'clock – and they don't usually finish until nine in the evening.

4 **Complete the table.**

name(s)	Miriam			Hector, Julio
job	secretary			
company			*Daily Record*	
working hours				6 a.m.– 9 p.m.
duties	answer telephone, speak to visitors, write letters, send faxes			

Language in Focus

Thinking about grammar
don't/doesn't (= do not/does not)

1 Read about Miriam, Kim, Hector and Julio again. Underline the sentences with **don't** and **doesn't**

2 Look at these examples and complete the table below.

a) I work in a factory. I don't work in an office.

b) You live in Rabat, I think. You don't live in Casablanca, do you?

c) Igor speaks English fluently. He doesn't speak French very well.

d) We start work at eight a.m. We don't finish until six p.m.

e) They study Engineering at home. They don't study at the Engineering Faculty.

I, you, we, they	_____	speak Spanish.
he, she	_____	

3 Complete these sentences with *don't* or *doesn't* and answer this question: 'What's George's job?'

I see George every day but I ① _____ know him very well. George ② _____ work in an office or a factory. If fact, he ③ _____ work inside a building. He stands in the street near my house. He ④ _____ have regular hours – he works when he wants to work. He sees

many people every day, but they ⑤ _____ talk to him very much. People buy something from him. It ⑥ _____ cost very much. George ⑦ _____ sell food or drink. He sells something that people read. But people ⑧ _____ keep it very long. They usually buy another one the next day.

4 Look at the table. It shows information about four people – Lee, Sarah, Toni and Hassan.

	drive a car	have a computer	speak French	work in an office
Lee	✗	✓	✓	✗
Sarah	✓	✗	✗	✓
Toni	✗	✓	✗	✓
Hassan	✓	✓	✗	✗

Complete the sentences about these people. For example:

Lee *doesn't drive* a car.

Lee *speaks* French.

Toni and Hassan *don't have* a computer.

a) Lee and Hassan _____ in an office.

b) Sarah _____ a computer.

c) Sarah and Hassan _____ a car.

d) Toni and Hassan _____ French.

e) Toni _____ a computer.

f) Sarah _____ in an office.

g) Lee and Toni _____ a car.

h) Sarah _____ French.

5 Write three sentences about Natasha and three sentences about Sam and Leo.

	have a mobile phone	speak German	work in a ministry
Natasha	✓	✓	✗
Sam and Leo	✗	✗	✓

Thinking about grammar
was/were

6 Complete the sentences below with **am**, **is** and **are**.

a) I _____ a secretary in the Sales Department. Before that I was a student at a business college.

b) Last year, Kim was a student at a college of journalism. Now he _____ a sports writer on one of Hong Kong's best newspapers.

c) Two years ago they were students at university. Now they _____ tour guides.

d) "Were you here last year?"

"No, I wasn't. I was still at school. This _____ my first year."

Was and were are the past simple forms of the verb 'to be'. Wasn't (was not) and weren't (were not) are the negative forms.

7 Maria and Sarah are talking about last year. Complete the dialogue with *was* or *were*.

M: Where ① _____ you at this time last year, Sarah?

S: This time last year? I ② _____ in India, I think.

M: That's right. You ③ _____ in Delhi, weren't you?

S: Yes. And my brother ④ _____ with me. It ⑤ _____ a great holiday. What about you?

M: I ⑥ _____ at work.

S: ⑦ _____ you? I don't remember.

M: Yes. We ⑧ _____ very busy at that time.

Telephoning

8 Listen to two telephone calls. Complete the conversations with these words and phrases.

> Ask him to call me   put me through
> speaking   This is   give him a message
> I'll phone again   My name's
> in a meeting   just a moment
> the line's busy

(**S** = switchboard, **N** = Nazeer, **M** = Michelle)

a) **S:** Good morning. NBW Electronics. Can I help you?

N: Hello. ① _____ Nazeer Khan. Can you ② _____ to the Sales Department, please?

S: Certainly, ③ _____. … I'm sorry, ④ _____. Would you like to hold?

N: It's OK. ⑤ _____ later.

b) **M:** Hello, Sales Department. Michelle ① _____.

N: Hello. ② _____ Nazeer. Can I speak to Amjad?

M: I'm sorry. He's ③ _____, Nazeer. Can I ④ _____?

N: Yes. ⑤ _____ as soon as possible.

M: Right. I'll tell him.

I'm sorry, he's in a very important meeting.

Skills in Focus – listening and speaking

Listening

1 Listen to a telephone call. The caller wants to leave a message. Complete the message form below.

New International University
Telephone message

Date: _____   Time: _____

Message for: _____

Name of caller: _____

Company: _____

Telephone number: _____

Message: _____

_____

_____

_____

Taken by: _____

Role play

2 Practise the dialogues on page 69 in pairs.

3 Practise leaving messages in pairs.

A: Caller. You want to speak to the people in the table below. Leave messages. Use these phrases:

Can I speak to … ?

Can you give him/her a message?

Tell him/her that …

Ask him/her to …

name	message
Dr Plantini	I'll phone again.
Mrs Clarkson	Please phone me as soon as possible.
Professor Norman	I can't come to the tutorial. I am sick.
Freda	I'm sorry.

B: Secretary. You work in the dean's office in the Faculty of Science. The people the caller wants to speak to are unavailable. Give reasons from the table below and take messages. Use these phrases:

… speaking.

I'm sorry, he/she's …

Can I give him/her a message?

	reason	message
Dr Plantini	On holiday.	
Mrs Clarkson	Busy on the other line.	
Professor Norman	In a lecture.	
Freda	Sick today.	

Presentation and discussion

4 Look at the picture of four people. Only three of them can stay in the boat. Work in groups of four. Each person should prepare a short presentation to say why their job is important and why they should stay in the boat.

5 Find out which of the four jobs the class think is the most important. Put the results on the chart below.

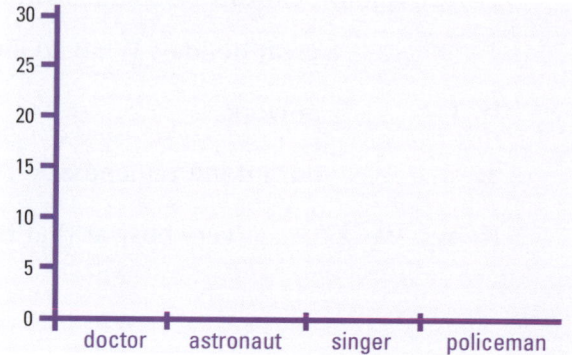

Skills in Focus – reading and writing

Reading

1 Discuss these questions in small groups.

a) How do people communicate with each other at work? Make a list of ways.

b) What makes a good communicator?

c) What is 'body language'? Give some examples.

d) Look at the people in the pictures. What can you learn from their body language?

2 Read the article about communication.

a) Check the list you made in 1a.

b) Check your definition of a good communicator.

c) What do these words and phrases mean: *message, face-to-face, positive, the receiver, feedback*?

d) What feelings do we show by our body language?

e) Complete the pie chart in the article.

Are you a good communicator?

We can all speak and write in our own language, so we can all communicate. Isn't that right? Well, no. It is true that most educated people can read and write, but that doesn't mean that they are good at communicating.

What, then, is a good communicator? Basically, it is someone who can get their message across clearly to another person – either by speaking or by writing.

Spoken communication may be face to face, as in a meeting or presentation, or it can be by phone, video, etc. Written communication is usually in the form of e-mails, memos, letters, reports and so on. We can also send a message to another person without written words or sounds. We do this by our 'body language'.

Body language means the way we sit, the expression on our face or the way we use our hands and arms. It shows our feelings, for example, if we are bored, upset or angry. Positive body language is important in spoken communication, too. It shows that you are interested in what you (or other people) are saying.

Good communications are especially important in the office. Every day we have to pass information or opinions to other people, either inside or outside the company. It is calculated that typical managers spend 44% of their time in face-to-face meetings and 22% on the telephone. They spend 12% of their time on written communication.

How can we be good communicators? First of all, we must think about the receiver – i.e., the person receiving the message. Who is he or she? What does he or she need to know? Secondly, it is important to make sure that the written or spoken message is clearly presented to the receiver. It should be the right length, not too long and not too short. If the message is spoken, use positive body language.

Finally, we must check that the receiver understands what we are saying. We can do this by getting 'feedback' from the receiver, for example, from a reply to our memo or letter, or through direct questions as we are speaking.

It is not enough to be able to speak and write a language. We must be able to communicate information and our ideas.

Sarah ~
A man phoned can you call him back?

Is this good communication? Why/why not?

3 Work with a partner to make a list of rules for good communication. Use the article to help you.

Writing

4 Choose one of the following and write a list of instructions on how to use it: *camera, fax machine, cassette recorder, mobile phone, washing machine.* Use the photocopier instructions on page 67 to help you.

5 Read the texts on page 67 again. Now choose one of the people in the table below. Write a paragraph about the person and his/her job.

name	Safak	Anna	Rex
home	Istanbul, Turkey	Rome, Italy	Manila, Philippines
job	salesman	hotel receptionist	car mechanic
company	Taba Shoes	Interhotel	Toyota
working hours	9 a.m.– 7 p.m., 6 days a week	6 a.m.– 2 p.m., or 2–10 p.m.	9 a.m.– 1 p.m., and 3–6 p.m.
duties	travel to different cities, visit customers	greet visitors, take telephone bookings	repair and service cars, clean new cars

6 Make notes about a friend or relative. What is his/her job? Where does he/she work? What are his/her working hours? What duties does he/she have? Now write a paragraph about him/her.

Study Skills and Review

Study Tip Improve your writing …

a) by reading

Good writing comes through reading practice. So read as much as you can – anything and everything.

It is important to read different types of texts. Which of these types of writing are interesting for you? Tick the boxes.

official letters ◯		personal letters ◯	
study notes ◯		diaries ◯	
reports ◯		lists ◯	
e-mails ◯		short stories ◯	
novels ◯		essays ◯	
instructions ◯		forms ◯	
memos ◯		poems ◯	

b) by checking

It is important to check your writing. Check:

- spelling
- punctuation
- word order
- articles (*a/an/the*)
- verb tense
- subject/verb agreement

Make a list of everything you read in English between now and this time next week. Make a note, too, of the time you spend reading. For example:

Date	Type of text	Time
4th May	English-language newspaper	10 mins.
5th May	Internet site on Chinese music	20 mins.

Vocabulary Review

Word families

A good way to organise vocabulary is by 'word families' – the parts of speech from one word. For example:

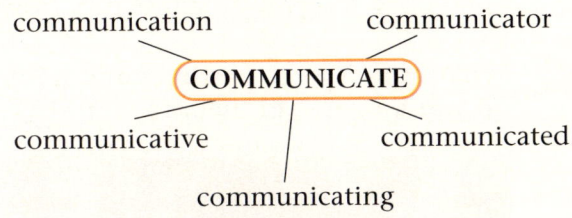

communication   communicator

COMMUNICATE

communicative   communicated

communicating

1 Make a word family for *tour*. Use a dictionary.

Work

2 Make spidergrams for:

a) office items

b) written communication

c) jobs

Grammar Review

• Present simple – negative forms

I You (sing.)	don't		
He, she, it	doesn't	work	in the city.
We You (plur.) They	don't		

• Present simple – spelling

The third-person form (*he, she* or *it*) of the present simple is made by adding *-s, -es* or *-ies*.

I work, I drive	He works, He drives
I go, I do	He goes, He does
I study, I cry	He studies, He cries

• Verb *to be* – present simple

I	am	We	are
You	are	You	are
He, She, It	is	They	are

I am a secretary in the Ministry of Information.

Yuki is a journalist for a national newspaper.

Photocopiers are very useful machines.

• Verb *to be* – past simple

I	was	We	were
You	were	You	were
He, She, It	was	They	were

I was a student at university two years ago.

Sarah and Mona were ill last week.

• Past time phrases

before that   last year/week/month

yesterday   two years/three days ago

Task 1: Write six true sentences about people you know using *was* and *were*.

Language Review

• Telephone language

This is … (speaking).	My name's …
I'll put you through.	Just a moment.
The line's busy.	I'll phone again.
Can I give him/her a message?	Could you give him/her a message?
Ask … to call me.	Can you put me through to … ?

Task 2: Write two dialogues between a secretary and a caller using the expressions above.

Introduction

Discussion

1 Look at the pictures of different activities. What are the people doing? Would you like to spend your free time like this? Why/why not?

2 Divide the activities in the box into two lists: 'sports' and 'pastimes and hobbies'.

computer games   gardening   reading
swimming   watching TV   tennis
cards   stamp collecting   astronomy
walking   basketball   cycling
listening to music   climbing
playing a musical instrument   camping

3 What other sports, pastimes and hobbies do you know? Add them to your lists.

A

B

C

D

Listing

4 Rosa and Lee are talking about their free time. Tick (✓) the activities they like and put a cross (✗) by the activities they don't like.

a) Rosa

walking ○

horse riding ○

reading ○

playing computer games ○

listening to music ○

watching TV ○

b) Lee

playing computer games ○

swimming ○

playing chess ○

playing football ○

cycling ○

collecting coins ○

Reading

5 Read the advertisement for 'Activity Holidays'. Choose two holidays that interest you and complete the application form with information about you.

ACTIVITY HOLIDAYS
Application form

(Please use BLOCK CAPITAL letters)

First name(s): _____

Family name: _____

Address: _____

_____

Tel: _____ Age: _____

Please send me details of the following holidays:

Adventure holidays: _____

_____

Study holidays: _____

_____

Activity Holidays

Do something different next summer.

**Do you hate sitting on the beach?
Do you feel bored watching television?
Do you like a challenge?
Do you enjoy taking a risk?
Yes? Then you are the type of person we want to hear from!**

At Activity Holidays we offer you a wide range of exciting adventure holidays – walking in beautiful forests, horse riding in the desert, camping in the mountains or bungee-jumping into river canyons.

Or if you prefer doing something rather quieter, we also organise study holidays. Perhaps you like learning languages or new skills such as computing, painting or pottery? We run holiday courses on these and many other skills.

To get more information on adventure or study holidays, complete the form opposite and send it to us at Activity Holidays. Or visit our website.

Just think, next year's holiday could be the best holiday you've ever had!

**Activity Holidays
PO Box 3409, Oslo, Norway
Website: www.activehols.ny**

Language in Focus

Thinking about grammar
love/like/hate/enjoy

1 Complete this paragraph with the '–ing' forms of these verbs: *travel, sit, walk, visit, drink.*

I love ① _____ Moscow in the winter. I like ② _____ in the parks when there is fresh snow and ③ _____ hot chocolate when I get home. But I don't like the summers very much. I hate ④ _____ in the hot Metro and don't enjoy ⑤ _____ in traffic jams when the temperature is in the 30s.

2 Look at the table about four students at the New International University. Complete the sentences about them. (love = ✓✓, like = ✓, not like/dislike = ✗, hate = ✗✗)

	write reports	listen to lectures	take exams	read in the library
Sarah	✓	✓	✗✗	✓✓
Bilal	✗	✓✓	✗	✓
Marina	✓	✓✓	✓	✓✓
George	✗✗	✗	✗✗	✗

For example:

Bilal and Marina love listening to lectures.
George doesn't like reading in the library.

a) Sarah and George _____ examinations.

b) Bilal _____ reports.

c) Sarah and Marina _____ library.

d) Marina _____ examinations.

e) Bilal _____ library.

f) George _____ lectures.

3 Work with a partner.
a) Complete the table with your likes and dislikes. (Use the code: love = ✓✓, like = ✓ etc.)

	write reports	listen to lectures	take exams	read in the library
You				
Your partner				

b) Ask a partner what he/she likes or dislikes at school, university or college.

For example:

A: Do you like writing reports?

B: No, I don't. I hate it.

A: And what about listening to lectures? Do you like that?

B: Yes. I quite like it.

Complete the second part of the table.

Vocabulary

4 Look at the pictures. Match the pictures with these feelings: *bored, excited, angry, afraid, sad, happy.*

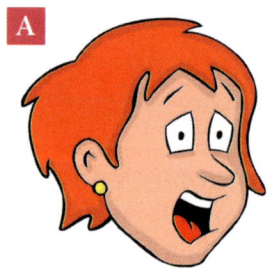

She feels _____.

He feels _____.

He feels _____.

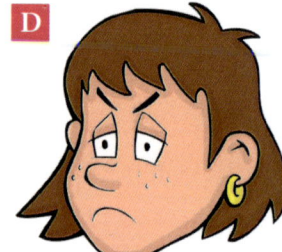

She feels _____.

She feels _____.

He feels _____.

Talking about the weather

5 Read these postcards from friends and match them with the holiday photos.

A *The weather today is quite hot and sunny, but there's a nice cool breeze. There are a few clouds in the sky. It's a beautiful day for going to the beach.*

B *I'm looking through the window of our room in the hotel. The weather is cloudy. The air is warm and rather humid. I think it's going to rain.*

C *The weather is very cold and sunny. There is a lot of snow on the ground, but it isn't snowing at the moment. I think I'll go out. I love walking in the snow.*

D *It's wet and windy today. It is raining fairly heavily. Unfortunately I have to go out in a few minutes and I haven't got an umbrella! I hate getting wet!*

E *The weather is awful! It's snowing hard and it's extremely cold. The sky is very dark. I'm going to stay in the hotel, near the fire!*

Intensifiers

Which word in this sentence is an intensifier?

The weather is very cold and sunny.

Very is an intensifier. Intensifiers come before an adjective (*cold, wet,* etc.). They tell us more about the adjective.

6 Read postcards A–E again. Underline all the intensifiers.

7 Talk about a) the weather today and b) the weather yesterday/last week. Use intensifiers and adjectives from the table in the phrases below.

intensifier	adjective
very (not very), fairly, extremely, quite, rather	cold, sunny, warm, hot, wet, cloudy, humid, dry, windy

It's _____ _____ today, isn't it?

Yes, it is. And it's _____ _____.

It was _____ _____ last week, wasn't it?

Yes, it was …

Skills in Focus – listening and speaking

Listening

1 How do you stay healthy? Discuss in a small group and make a list of ways. Use imperatives, e.g., 'Eat plenty of fresh fruit.' 'Don't smoke.'

2 Listen to an interview. Mary Aboni is a famous marathon runner. She is in a TV studio, talking about how she spends a holiday.

a) Put the pictures below in the right order (1–6).

b) Mary talks about two things that are important for athletes to do. What are they?

Speaking

3 Interview another student about holidays. Then change roles.

Student A: The interviewer. Ask your partner how he/she spends the holidays. Find out what he/she likes to do. Make a note of his/her answers.

Student B: Answer the interviewer's questions.

Survey

4 In groups, collect all the information about holidays from students in the class. Find out what their favourite activities are. Put the results in a bar chart.

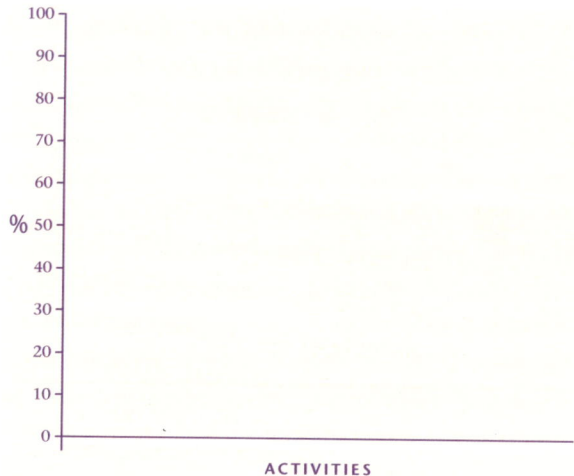

Presentation

5 You work for a holiday company in your country, like 'Activity Holidays'. Prepare a short presentation about the company and the holidays it offers. Give the talk to a group of students.

Skills in Focus – reading and writing

Reading

1 Work in pairs. What do you want to know about hurricanes?

a) Write five 'wh-' questions about hurricanes.

b) Read the encyclopaedia entry and try to find answers to your questions.

2 Match the headings below to paragraphs A–E.

- How do hurricanes begin?
- The names of hurricanes
- What is a hurricane?
- The eye of the storm
- Damage and destruction

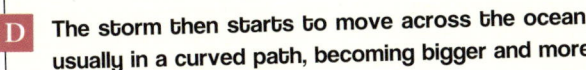

HURRICANES

A Hurricane is the name given to an extremely powerful tropical storm or cyclone occurring in the Atlantic Ocean. In the Pacific Ocean, hurricanes are known as typhoons. These storms have winds of more than 120 km/hour and sometimes as much as 250 km/hour. They can cover a wide area, up to 480 kilometres across.

B At the centre of the storm is 'the eye', an area of quiet winds and clear skies. Here the air pressure is at the lowest point. The eye is usually about 24 kilometres across.

C Hurricanes form in the oceans near the Equator. In these areas, winds are usually very light and the air is warm and humid. Sometimes the air in these regions mixes with cold, denser air. The cold air forces the warm air upwards, the pressure falls, and the storm begins to develop.

D The storm then starts to move across the ocean, usually in a curved path, becoming bigger and more powerful. When it reaches land it can cause a lot of damage to property and flooding. This is because of the strong winds and heavy rain that come with hurricanes. The winds produce very rough seas that are a danger to shipping and can damage coastal areas. Eventually, as it moves into cooler regions, the hurricane loses its strength and dies out.

E In the Atlantic, the hurricane season is from April to November, with the peak of the season in September. At the start of the season, each hurricane is given a name. The first of the season begins with A, the second with B, and so on (for example, Andrew, Bertha …). In 1999, there was a very big hurricane called Floyd. This caused a lot of damage to the Bahamas and the east coast of the United States.

Writing

3 Choose one of the following natural phenomena: *tornado, hailstorm, tidal wave, flood, earthquake*. Find information about it and write a short definition.

Reading and writing

4 Read this article about Tony, who wants to be a student representative for his college. Complete the paragraph with appropriate verbs in the '–ing' form.

> Tony is a student at the Ocean College of Science and Technology. He likes sport very much, and in his free time he enjoys ① _____ basketball with friends. His favourite team is the Hornets. If the weather is fine, he goes ② _____ in the sea or he takes his tent and goes ③ _____ in the mountains for a couple of days. He's also a member of a karate club and goes there twice a week. Tony loves ④ _____ stamps. He has hundreds of stamps from all over the world. However, Tony doesn't like ⑤ _____ TV very much and he hates ⑥ _____ to the cinema. When he wants to relax, he usually reads a novel or surfs the Internet.

5 Choose one of these people. Using the notes, write about their likes and dislikes.

Walter: student – technical college

Likes: walking, cycling (member of Cycling Club), watching TV, listening to rock music (the Pugs – his favourite band), playing chess (was school champion), surfing the Internet

Dislikes: aerobics, going to gym, reading, rap music

Mimi: secretary – bank

Likes: tennis (plays every day), cycling (cycles to work), swimming, reading, visiting museums and art galleries (during holidays) (Monet – her favourite painter), listening to radio (while doing housework)

Dislikes: computer games, TV, jogging, driving

Study Skills and Review

Study Tip | A good listener prepares and predicts …

1) Before you listen to something in English, for example, a lecture, try to prepare yourself. Read about the topic. Make sure you know the important vocabulary.

2) While you listen, try to predict what the speaker is going to say. Use:
   - intonation
   - signals (*I like the idea, but …*)
   - connectors (*On the other hand …*)

1 You are going to listen to the first part of a talk on avalanches.

a) Before you listen: What do you know about avalanches? What words and phrases will you hear? Make a list with a partner.

b) Listen to the talk and complete the outline below. How does the lecturer explain the structure of the talk? How does his speech change when he has something important to say?

> ### AVALANCHES
>
> Q1: _____
>
> _____
>
> Q2: _____
>
>   a) _____
>
>   b) _____
>
>   c) _____
>
>   d) _____
>
> Q3: _____

Vocabulary Review

Temperature

1 Put these adjectives in order, starting with the coldest: *cold, hot, freezing, cool, warm, boiling.*

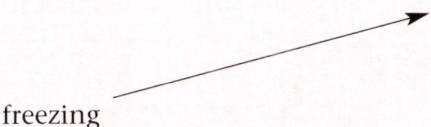

freezing

Adjectives

2 Put these adjectives in order:

a) *good, lovely, bad, wonderful, terrible, fine, poor*

b) *big, small, huge, tiny, large*

Activities

3 Complete the table with activities from the unit. Add others that you know.

	indoors	outdoors
sports	billiards bowling	football running
pastimes and hobbies	stamp collecting listening to music	camping walking

4 Which verb goes with which activity? Write *play* or *go* in the spaces below.

_____ camping	_____ the piano
_____ cards	_____ swimming
_____ basketball	_____ horse riding

Feelings

Task 1: Write three sentences using verbs and activities from the table.

5 Make a spidergram for *feelings* (*bored, happy*, etc.).

Grammar Review

- ### The –*ing* form

We use the '–ing' form after verbs such as *like, love, hate, enjoy* and *dislike.*

> We **enjoy** swimm**ing**.

> He **hates** visit**ing** museums.

Task 2: Write five true sentences about people you know.

For example:

Nina hates playing computer games.

I love walking in the rain.

- ### Intensifiers

article	intensifier	adjective	noun
a(n)	extremely	good	film
	really	nice	day
	rather	bad	book
	quite	beautiful	picture
	fairly	interesting	hotel

Task 3: Reorder the sentences.

a) nice a really that's photograph !

b) the food with we at restaurant weren't happy very the .

c) her extremely results examination were good .

Language Review

- ### Talking about the weather

It's	extremely	hot	today.
	very	cold	
It was	quite	wet	yesterday.
	not very	humid	last week.
		windy	

It's	raining	heavily.
	snowing	hard.

The weather's	wonderful	today.
	nice	in June.
	fine	at this time of the year.
	lovely	

Introduction

Discussion

1 Match the sentences with the pictures.

A I always shake hands with friends when we meet.

B It is friendly to use a person's first name as soon as you are introduced.

C It's always important to wear clothes you feel comfortable in.

D I never give tips. It's unnecessary.

E I usually take presents when I am invited to a friend's house for dinner.

F If I have an appointment I am never more than half an hour late.

G I like to find out everything about a person when we meet.

2 Now discuss the sentences in groups. Do you agree or disagree with them? Why or why not?

3 Look at the situation in the cartoon below. What would you do in this situation:

a) if you were the guest?

b) if you were the host?

Listening

4 Four students are talking about their study routines. Listen and make notes in the table.

	when	where	how
Samira			
Joe			
Kate			
Ahmed			

Reading

5 These people are writing about their cultures. Match the person with their paragraph.

Mark – Australia

Badria – Kuwait

Karl – Germany

Chantelle – France

A People from other countries think we are very formal. For example, I work in an office. Every morning before I start work I have to greet my colleagues. I shake hands with all my male colleagues and I kiss my female colleagues on both cheeks.

B Being punctual is very important in my culture. We are never late. If you are late for an appointment, even just a few minutes, people think you are very rude. If you are late for a meeting, people also think you are not very serious about your work.

C I think we are very hospitable people. When we have visitors we always treat them very well because they are our guests. At home we always make them feel welcome and we offer them food and drink. This is our custom.

D I think we are quite friendly people. We aren't very formal when we meet. We like to use a person's first name when we are introduced. In this way we show them that we want to be friendly. We never worry about how important a person is – we like to think that everyone is equal.

6 What about your culture? Are you formal when you meet people? Are you hospitable to strangers? Are you punctual for meetings? Tick the boxes and discuss in groups.

	extremely	very	quite	not very
formal	○	○	○	○
hospitable	○	○	○	○
punctual	○	○	○	○
friendly	○	○	○	○

Language in Focus

Thinking about grammar
Adverbs of frequency:
always, usually, often, sometimes, never

 Circle the adverbs of frequency in these sentences. Do they come before or after the verb? Can you work out any rules?

a) I always have breakfast at 7.00.

b) What's happened? Martha is never late.

c) They usually take presents for the host.

d) Peter is always in the library!

e) Sometimes I feel like singing.

f) Kate never studies in the evening.

g) We sometimes watch TV in the afternoon.

h) In my country, people don't often shake hands.

i) Librans are usually rather artistic.

j) I often give a tip to a taxi driver.

Adverbs of frequency usually go before the verb …

> I **always** work late.

> She **usually** works late.

> They **sometimes** work late.

… but they go after the verb 'to be'.

> You are **often** ill.

> He is **never** ill.

Adverbs of frequency come after auxiliary verbs such as *don't*, *doesn't*, *can* and *will*.

> I don't **usually** work late.

> She doesn't **always** arrive on time.

Usually and **sometimes** can also go at the beginning of a sentence.

> **Usually** we work late on Thursdays.

> **Sometimes** I study in the library.

 Put the adverbs of frequency in the correct place in these sentences.

a) My son and I go fishing at the weekend. (always)

b) It is cold in Muscat in the winter. (never)

c) I don't speak English outside the college. (usually)

d) Marina listens to music in her car. (sometimes)

e) Our buses are late and overcrowded. (always)

f) Sam doesn't study very hard. (often)

g) Ahmed smokes in his car. (never)

h) I use the computer to send e-mails. (sometimes)

i) People in Japan bow when they meet. (often)

j) Hannan is a few minutes early for meetings. (usually)

 Write six sentences about these people.

	Maria	Altaf
get up/early/in the morning	usually	never
study/in the library	always	often
work/in the evening	usually	sometimes
have/breakfast	never	always
play/chess/at the weekend	sometimes	usually
walk/to the college	often	never

For example:

Maria usually gets up early in the morning.

Altaf never gets up early in the morning.

Describing routines

 **Joe is talking to Salem about an examination. Listen to their conversation and answer the questions below.**

a) What examination is Joe worried about?

b) What is the first thing Salem does when he prepares for an exam?

c) Salem thinks exercise is important. Why?

5 **Listen again and complete the dialogue with words and phrases from the box.**

> **Finally   never   And after that   as**
> **always   first of all   Then   usually**

S: Hi, Joe. How are you?

J: OK, but I'm a bit worried.

S: Oh, what about?

J: The Biology examination.

S: Are you ready for it?

J: No, I'm not. I haven't done a thing yet. How do you prepare for an exam, Salem?

S: Well, ① _____, I make a study timetable for the week.

J: I ② _____ do that.

S: You should. It's very useful. ③ _____ I usually go through my lecture notes. First I read them quickly and then I rewrite them.

J: Rewrite them? That takes a lot of time, doesn't it? I've got a lot of notes.

S: Yes, but it's useful. ④ _____ I rewrite my notes, I understand everything better.

J: Hmm. ⑤ _____?

S: Well, then I ⑥ _____ look at the main textbooks.

J: I don't have time to do that.

S: But I just read the main parts of the books – and I ⑦ _____ use a highlighter. I mark the important points.

J: I see. And what else?

S: ⑧ _____, I make sure I get a lot of exercise. Oxygen is good for the brain.

J: Yes, I remember! We studied that in Biology!

> **Asking about and describing routines**
>
> How do you ... (study/spend your time)?
>
> What do you do first?
>
> What next?
>
> What do you do after that?
>
> And then?
>
> First ...   Then ...   After that ...   Finally ...

6 **How do you prepare for an examination? Discuss with a partner. Use the phrases in the box and adverbs of frequency.**

Vocabulary

7 **Which verbs collocate with the nouns in the table? Put ticks in the correct columns.**

	shake	wear	use	have	give
first names					
clothes					
tips					
hands					
a meeting					

8 **Complete these sentences with verb + noun combinations from the table.**

a) In my country, men never _____ with women when they meet.

b) We don't usually _____ to taxi drivers.

c) If you _____ with someone, it is important to be on time.

d) When I am introduced to older people, I never _____. I always say 'Mr' or 'Mrs'.

e) Students usually _____ informal _____ to the college, for example, T-shirts and jeans.

Skills in Focus – listening and speaking

Listening

1 What holidays are there in your country? Make a list. What type of holiday is each one – religious, national, etc.?

2 Listen to part of a lecture about holidays and festivals and complete the notes.

> ### Holidays and festivals
>
> The word holiday = '_____ day'
>
> Holidays are: a) _____
>
>   b) secular (non-religious)
>
> <u>Types of holiday:</u>
>
> a) spring holidays, e.g., _____ in Iran
>
> b) harvest festivals, e.g., _____ in _____
>
> c) days to honour _____ , e.g., in _____
>
> d) _____ , e.g., Jordan – 25ᵗʰ May
>
> e) Holidays to honour _____ , e.g., in
>
>   India, 2ⁿᵈ October, the birthday
>
>   of _____
>
> f) _____ in Russia, _____ March.
>
> <u>Holidays are important because</u>
>
> 1) they are a tonic
>
> 2) they remind people of the _____

Saying the date

We say the date in two different ways.

2ⁿᵈ March = "The second of March"

            or "March the second"*

How are dates pronounced in the lecture about holidays and festivals?

*In US English, the pronunciation is "March second".

3 Think of some important dates in your life (birthdays, anniversaries, etc.). Work in pairs. Tell your partner the dates, varying your pronunciation.

Speaking

4 Choose one of the holidays or festivals in your country and make notes about it. When is it? How old is it? What usually happens?

5 Work in groups. Describe the festival to your group.

6 A group of foreign visitors is coming to visit your country.

  a) Make a list of things they need to know about customs in your country.

  b) Give a short talk about the customs of your country for the visitors.

Skills in Focus – reading and writing

Reading

1 Look at this picture. What do you think these people are doing and why?

2 Now read about the festival. Choose headings for paragraphs A–F from the list below.

- What are the rules?
- Conclusion
- History of the festival
- Introduction
- Preparations on the day
- What is La Tomatina?

3 Look at the underlined words. Match them with these meanings:

a) materials used in war

b) to squeeze or flatten until soft

c) ready to eat

d) unplanned

e) dirty

f) very big

g) to come together slowly

h) something to aim or shoot at

La Tomatina

A Imagine the scene. You are in a small Spanish town. The streets are full of hundreds of people. There are thousands of kilos of ripe tomatoes and you can throw them at anyone you want. Does this sound like fun … or is it your idea of hell?

B It's strange but true. Every year, on the last Wednesday in August, the town of Buñol in eastern Spain becomes a battlefield for two hours. From 11 in the morning until one o'clock in the afternoon, the residents and visitors throw ripe tomatoes at each other. It is the 'tomato war' known as La Tomatina.

C There is no religious or political meaning to this unusual festival. It began in 1944 as a small impromptu tomato fight between friends. Since then, it has grown into a huge event in which the whole town participates. More than twenty thousand people crowd into the main square and the streets around it. Thousands of kilos of tomatoes are brought in by lorries from Extremadura in the west of Spain especially for the festival.

D During the morning, the shopkeepers cover the fronts of their shops with plastic sheets. Then young people start to gather in the main square. Buckets of water are thrown at the crowd to get things started. Next, trucks loaded with 'ammunition' roll into the square and people seated on the trucks start to throw tomatoes at the crowds below. Then the fight begins.

E The rules are simple: you can only use tomatoes and you must squash them before throwing them. Anyone can join in, including visitors from outside. But if you are thinking of coming, make sure you are wearing old clothes. Tourists with cameras are a special target. Don't even think of washing your clothes afterwards.

F La Tomatina is just part of a week-long festival in Buñol. There are musical bands, fireworks and food. It is a week of messy fun!

Writing

4 An Iranian student is writing about a spring festival in his country, Now-Rouz, for the student magazine. Complete the text with words from the box.

> put   usually   end   happy
> traditions   wear   festival   wish
> covers   celebrate   when

Now-Rouz _____

My favourite festival in Iran is Now-rouz, or New Year. It is a festival to ① _____ the arrival of spring. It takes place at the ② _____ of March ③ _____ the winter snows disappear and flowers start to appear.

During the festival, people ④ _____ new clothes and they ⑤ _____ clean their houses. It is a time when we greet our friends and neighbours and ⑥ _____ them a happy New Year.

One of the ⑦ _____ at Now-rouz is that every family ⑧ _____ a table with a cloth. We ⑨ _____ seven things beginning with 's' on the table. These are greenery (sabzi), an apple (sib), vinegar (serkeh), garlic (sir), a gold or silver piece (sekeh), a spice (somaq) and a sweet dish (samanu).

Now-rouz is a wonderful family ⑩ _____. Everyone is very ⑪ _____ that winter is over.

5 Write a short article about a festival in your country. Use the notes you made earlier.

6 Write an e-mail to a friend. Describe how you study for an exam.

Study Skills and Review

Study Tip   Take good notes!

Good notes are important for reading and for listening.

Rules for making notes. Make sure that:

1) the information is correct.

2) you only have important information.

3) the notes are organised clearly.

4) you use abbreviations where possible.

Why use notes?

1) They help you read or listen better.

2) You can use them for exam revision.

3) You can add information to them.

What do these abbreviations mean? Use a dictionary to find out.

> ed.   cf.   ref.   info.   e.g.   etc.
> 1st   m   cm   km   kg

1 Read the article about La Tomatina again and make notes about the festival.

2 Compare your notes with three other people. Are your notes better than the others? What do you think makes good notes?

Vocabulary Review

Prefixes

1 Here are some adjectives from the unit. Use prefixes (*in-*, *un-*, *im-*, etc.) to make the opposite forms.

adjective	opposite
formal	
friendly	
hospitable	
polite	
necessary	
important	

Holidays

2 Complete the spidergram.

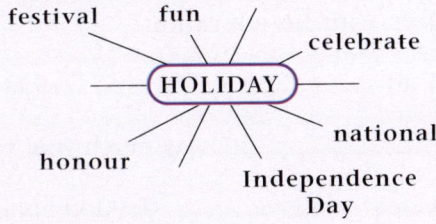

festival   fun

celebrate

HOLIDAY

national

honour

Independence Day

Routines

3 These words describe a daily routine. Add more to the list: *get up, have (breakfast, tea), walk, watch, ...*

4 Add to this list of verbs related to a study routine: *read, read through, study, look at, take notes, prepare, ...*

Grammar Review

- **Adverbs of frequency**

always

usually

often

sometimes

never

> We **often** work late.
>
> I am **often** ill.
>
> She doesn't **often** arrive on time.

Task 1: Write six sentences to describe what you do on holiday or a weekend. Use adverbs of frequency and time phrases (see Unit 2).

Task 2: Write six similar sentences about someone you know.

Language Review

- **Describing routines**

first of all ...

then ...

next ...

after that ...

finally ...

- **Asking about routines**

How do you ... (study/spend your time)?

What do you do first?

What next?

And then?

What do you do after that?

Task 3: Write a dialogue between a journalist and a famous sportsperson/musician about how he or she prepares himself/herself for a match/event/concert.

Listening: Part 1

1 You are going to listen to a radio phone-in programme where people can phone and ask experts for advice. Read the question, then listen and find the correct answer.

The programme is about:

a) choosing and buying computers for children.

b) using computers for games and Internet access.

c) using computers in the classroom.

d) choosing the best software for your computer.

2 Listen again and decide if the sentences below are true or false.

a) Mrs White isn't sure about buying her son a computer.

b) Richard believes a home computer will help children with their general education.

c) A new computer for word processing, Internet access and educational programs costs about £400.

d) A new computer for all the basics, most games and desktop publishing costs a lot more.

e) Speed and power are not as important as reliability.

f) Richard advises Mrs White to choose the computer first, then the software.

g) You will need to spend more money on your computer after you have bought it.

Language in Focus: Questions

3 Listen again and complete Mrs White's questions.

a) _____ to buy one to help him with his education?

b) Can _____ what to buy?

c) _____ how much that will cost?

d) Could you give _____ desktop publishing?

e) _____ decide what's important?

f) What exactly _____?

Listening: Part 2

 Try to fill in the missing words in the extract from Mr Byte's talk. Then listen and check your answers.

Extract 1

Don't let your technophobia put you off learning about computers and helping your children.

Real learning happens in two ways: one is active, where children learn by doing and experimenting; the second is where children think about what they have done. So even if you ① _____ understand computers, you can help, ② _____ _____ _____ by asking children to show you what they are doing, ③ _____ talk about how and why they did it. And ④ _____ _____, you can ask them what they have discovered. This is similar to discussing a book with your child.

Remember, children like ⑤ _____ things and talking about what they have done; they ⑥ _____ _____ _____ to lectures!

Extract 2

If you buy a computer, you need to learn some of the basics. So put the computer in a room that all the family uses, not your child's bedroom.

Don't buy a computer for the children; buy one for the family to share. Some computers and software are ⑦ _____ expensive. But it is ⑧ _____ to pay a lot of money. A secondhand one is ⑨ _____ all right for educational use; and remember – sending e-mails is much faster and ⑩ _____ _____ ordinary mail, or 'snail mail', as computer whiz kids say!

Extract 3

It ⑪ _____ _____ better to be honest with your children. So start by telling your children you can see the value of a computer and you want to learn to use it with them. Many schools and libraries ⑫ _____ computer clubs that give children access to computers outside the school day. Some clubs allow children and parents to learn together.

⑬ _____, you ⑭ _____ also learn the basics from the many books, magazines and courses that are available. They ⑮ _____ _____ very helpful articles for beginners, as well as more experienced computer users. You'll soon become a 'technomaniac' instead of a 'technophobe'!

Language in Focus:
Collocation and prefixes

 Match each adjective to a suitable noun.

a) national	1) stapler
b) beautiful	2) celebration
c) growing	3) communication
d) tourist	4) economy
e) birthday	5) location
f) office	6) village
g) dry	7) traditions
h) long	8) population
i) electronic	9) distance
j) mountain	10) climate

6 Choose the correct form of the word to go in each sentence.

un/important	in/formal
un/friendly	in/hospitable
un/necessary	un/punctual
un/interesting	dis/honour

Example: un/offical

There was an <u>unofficial</u> celebration after we won the football match. We all decided to go the Happy Meal restaurant.

a) The people of this village are very

_____.They will give you food

and drink if you need it.

b) You must wear a shirt and tie to that

restaurant; it's very _____.

c) He lost his job because he wasn't very

_____. One day he was nearly an

hour late for work!

d) Nobody likes her because she's so

_____.

e) It's _____ to clean your car

every day.

f) It's _____ to do a little revision

every day.

g) He brought _____ to his family –

he stole money from his employer.

h) I nearly fell asleep when I read that book –

it's really _____.

 Reading

The paragraphs here come from three different articles. Article A is about communications, B is about a Spanish festival and C is about e-mails.

a) **Find the paragraphs from each article and letter them A, B and C.**

b) **Number the paragraphs from each article in order, e.g., A1, A2, A3.**

Imagine the scene. You are in a small Spanish town. The streets are full of hundreds of people. There are thousands of kilos of ripe tomatoes and you can throw them at anyone you want. Does this sound like fun … or is it your idea of hell?

It's strange but true. Every year, on the last Wednesday in August, the town of Buñol in eastern Spain becomes a battlefield for two hours. From 11 in the morning until one o'clock in the afternoon, the residents and visitors throw ripe tomatoes at each other. It is the 'tomato war' known as *La Tomatina*.

Spoken communication may be face-to-face, as in a meeting or presentation, or it can be by phone, video, etc. Written communication is usually in the form of e-mails, memos, letters, reports and so on. We can also send a message to another person without written words or sounds. We do this by our 'body language'.

There is no religious or political meaning to this unusual festival. It began in 1944 as a small impromptu tomato fight between friends. Since then, it has grown into a huge event in which the whole town participates. More than twenty thousand people crowd into the main square and the streets around it. Thousands of kilos of tomatoes are brought in by lorries from Extremadura in the west of Spain especially for the festival.

To use e-mail, you need three things. First, of course, you need a computer with a modem. Secondly, you need to have an e-mail application (such as Netscape Messenger), and thirdly, you need to know the address of the person you are writing to. An e-mail address is written on one line. It looks like this: colleges@gto.net.om. We read the address in this way: "colleges at gto dot net dot om". (We read abbreviations like 'gto' letter by letter. We read words like 'colleges' and 'net' in full.)

We can all speak and write in our own languages, so we can all communicate. Isn't that right? Well, no. It is true that most educated people can read and write, but that doesn't mean that they are good at communicating.

What if there was a third way that was both fast and cheap? Well, there is. It is called e-mail, and it will change your life. E-mail (electronic mail) is a way of sending messages from one computer to another. The message you type on your computer will probably appear on the screen of your friend in New York in minutes. The message can be ordinary writing, or you can attach pictures (graphics), photographs and even sounds to your message.

What, then, is a good communicator? Basically, it is someone who can get their message across clearly to another person – either by speaking or by writing.

You live in Bangkok but you want to send messages to a friend who is studying in New York. What do you do? Do you phone and then get very high telephone bills (and maybe wake your friend up in the middle of the night)? Or do you send letters and wait for weeks and weeks to get a reply? The first way is fast but expensive. The second (sometimes called 'snail mail') is cheap but slow.

 8 Here is the next paragraph from text A above.

Complete the text with a word from the box in each numbered space.

angry arms face saying sit spoken

Body language means the way we ① _____, the expression on our ② _____ or the way we use our hands and ③ _____. It shows our feelings, for example, if we are bored, upset or ④ _____. Positive body language is important in ⑤ _____ communication, too. It shows that you are interested in what you (or other people) are ⑥ _____.

 9 Here is the next paragraph from text B above.

Number the sentences and phrases in the correct order.

____ and people seated on the trucks start to throw tomatoes at the crowds below.

____ Buckets of water are thrown at the crowd to get things started.

____ During the morning, the shopkeepers cover the fronts of their shops with plastic sheets.

____ Next, trucks loaded with 'ammunition' roll into the square

____ Then the fight begins.

____ Then young people start to gather in the main square.

10 In the next paragraph from text C above, the writer explains how to send an e-mail message. Read and correct the explanation below.

To send a message, select 'File' from the menu of your e-mail. Then type in the name of the person you are sending the message to and the date of the message. Finally, type your message, point the computer to the 'Send' icon and tick. If you want to reply to a message, just click on the 'Receive' icon.

Introduction

Discussion

1 Look at the diagrams and discuss the questions in groups.

A Books published annually

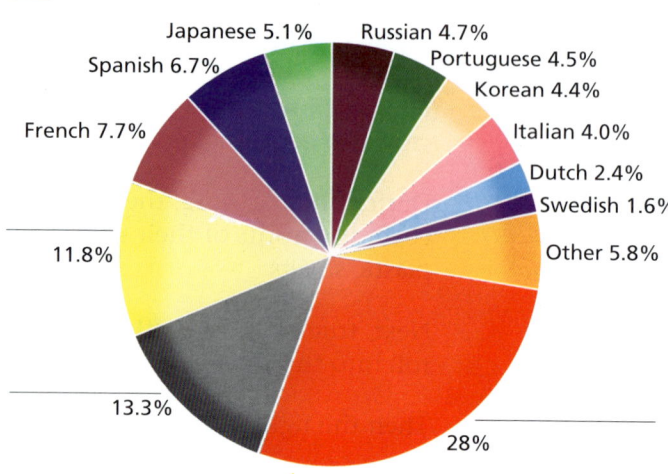

Japanese 5.1% Russian 4.7%
Spanish 6.7% Portuguese 4.5%
Korean 4.4%
French 7.7%
Italian 4.0%
Dutch 2.4%
Swedish 1.6%
11.8%
Other 5.8%
13.3%
28%

a) What are the three missing languages?

B

Home pages on the World Wide Web in English

	Language	Estimated Servers	%
1			84.3
2			4.5
3			3.1
4	French	7,213	1.8
5	Spanish	4,646	1.2
6	Swedish	4,279	1.1
7	Italian	3,790	1.0
8	Portuguese	2,567	0.7
9	Dutch	2,445	0.6
10	Norwegian	2,323	0.6

b) Which languages are in the first three positions?

C

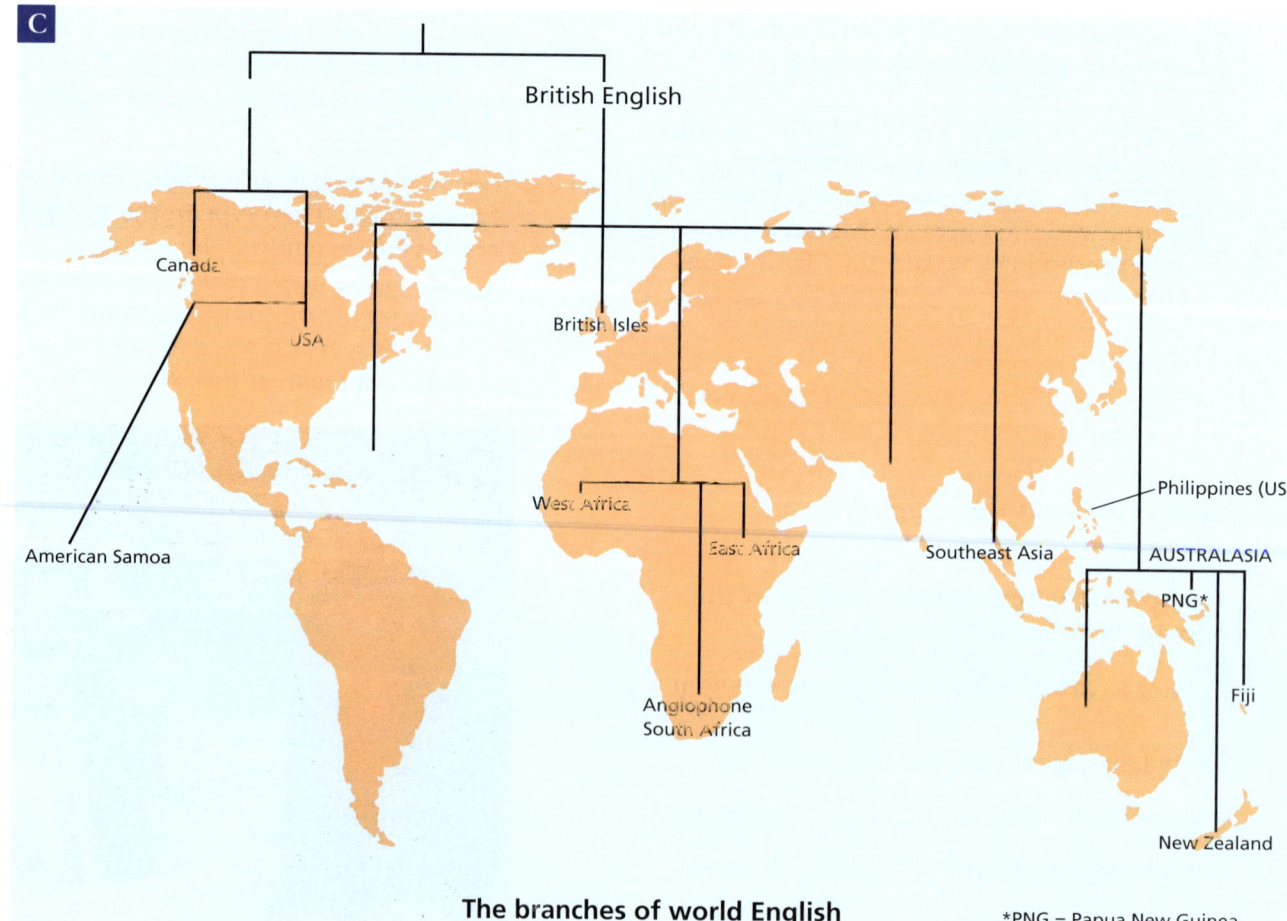

British English

Canada

USA

British Isles

West Africa

American Samoa

East Africa

Southeast Asia

Philippines (US)

AUSTRALASIA

PNG*

Fiji

Anglophone South Africa

New Zealand

The branches of world English   *PNG = Papua New Guinea

c) Complete the classification with words from the box.

> Caribbean   American English
> South Asia   Australia

d) Which features of these types of English are different? (e.g., pronunciation, ...)

Listening

2 **Sarah is interviewing three students about the status of English in their countries. Listen and complete the table.**

	Afzal	**Elizabeth**	**Victor**
country			
status of English	official language		
other			minority languages

3 **Listen again and say if these sentences are true or false.**

a) India has two official languages.

b) Afzal doesn't speak Urdu at home.

c) The people of the Bahamas speak English as their native language.

d) The Bahamas are a British colony.

e) Elizabeth can speak French fluently.

f) English has official status in Russia.

g) Victor works as an interpreter.

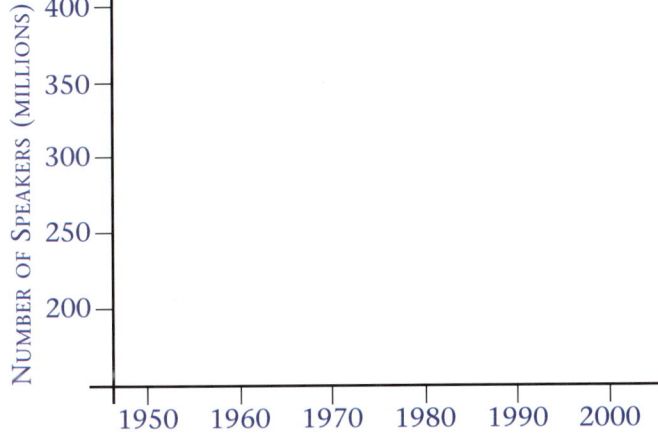

4 **Listen to a lecturer talking about the number of English speakers in the world.**

a) Find out the number of speakers of English in 1950, 1970 and 2000.

b) Mark the totals on the graph and draw the curve.

Reading

5 **Read about the status of English in the Philippines, Canada and Tunisia.**

a) Match the paragraphs with the countries.

b) Find the countries on the map on page 94.

A) _____

> Our country used to be a British colony, and so for many years English was the only official language. Now we have two official languages: French and English. We also have a number of minority languages. In some parts of the country education is in English and in other parts it is in French. We have a bilingual system.

B) _____

> The official language of our country is Arabic, although many people use French in business and education. A small number of people also speak the Berber language. English is taught in schools as a foreign language, but it is becoming more and more important.

C) _____

> Our country was a Spanish colony for more than 200 years. Spanish used to be the official language, but now only a small number of people can speak Spanish. The official language is Tagalog. However, English is widely used as a second language in business, education and government. There are also several other languages and dialects.

Language in Focus

Past time: **last, ago, in**	
last	year month week
six years five minutes two days a long time	**ago**
in	March 1998 the 20th century

1 Complete the sentences with past time words.

a) _____ year I was a student at secondary school in Indonesia.

b) The total number of English speakers was 200 million _____ 1950.

c) Hassan couldn't speak a word of English five years _____.

2 Look at the pictures below and talk about the people with a partner. Use *was/were* and *last, ago* or *in*.

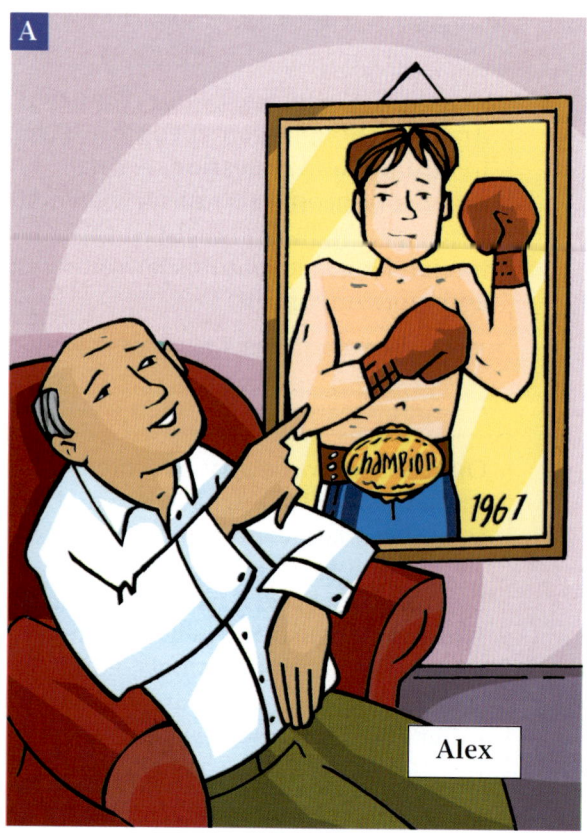

A

Alex

B

Sam

Pili

last summer

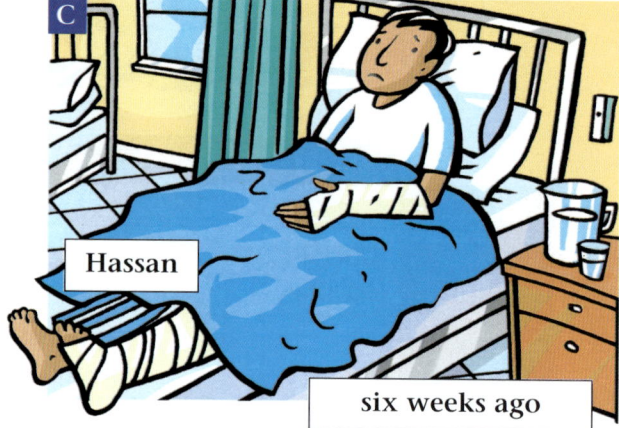

C

Hassan

six weeks ago

Vocabulary

3 Match the country with the official language.

Countries

Argentina   Brazil   Australia

Nigeria   Senegal   Sudan   Taiwan

Yemen   Pakistan   Austria

Iran   Cuba   Jamaica   Kenya

Angola   the Netherlands

Languages

French   Dutch   German

English   Spanish   Portuguese

Arabic   Chinese   Swahili

Portuguese   Arabic   Urdu   English

Farsi   English   Spanish

4 What are the official languages of these countries? Put them in the table: China, Japan, Turkey, Italy, Kuwait, Russia, United Kingdom, Sweden, Greece, Mozambique, Hungary, Thailand.

-ish	-ese	-ian	other

Percentages

We say percentages like this:

55% = "fifty-five per cent"

12.5% = "twelve point five per cent"

5 Choose five of these percentages. Dictate them to a partner.

43%	16.9%	70.5%	94%	8.5%
60.8%	41%	87.4%	30%	24.3%

Thinking about grammar
can/can't (can not/cannot)

6 Put the words below in the correct order to make sentences with **can** and **can't**.

a) languages/I/five/speak/can .

b) speak/you/Farsi/can ?

c) what/understand/saying/can't/I/he's .

d) but/she/Chinese/it/speak/write/can/can't/Sheila .

could/couldn't (could not)

7 **Read the examples below and complete this sentence.**

Could(n't) is the _____ form of **can('t)**.

a) I could speak Spanish quite well a few years ago, but now I speak it very badly.

b) Lee couldn't understand a word of French last year, but now he is almost fluent.

Note: the modals *can* and *could* come before the main verb.

Making requests

8 Listen and complete the dialogues.

a) **A:** Excuse me. _____ sit here?

   B: Yes, _____. It's free.

b) **A:** Er … Maria.

   B: Yes?

   A: I haven't got any money. _____ lend me ten dollars?

   B: Ten dollars? _____. I've only got two.

c) **A:** Excuse me. _____ borrow your pen?

   B: _____.

d) **A:** Er … Tom. I have to go to the airport tomorrow.

   B: What time?

   A: Six o'clock in the morning. _____ give me a lift?

   B: _____ I have to go to the dentist's tomorrow morning. Sorry.

9 Put these requests in order of politeness, beginning with the most polite.

a) What's the time?

b) Can you tell me the time?

c) Tell me the time.

d) Could you possibly tell me the time?

e) Could you tell me the time, please?

Skills in Focus – listening and speaking

Survey

1 Interview four people. Ask them about the languages they speak and complete the table. Find out about their level (very good, good, basic) for speaking (S), and for reading and writing (R/W).

Which languages do you speak?
What's your native language?
How well do you speak English?

For example:

name	native language	second language	other languages
Latifa	Arabic	French (S: v. good, R/W: good)	English (S: good, R/W: basic)

Listening and note-taking

2 Listen to Professor Selina. She is talking about the three types of English speaker. Complete the notes and the diagram opposite.

Three types of English speaker

1) _____

They live in _____

where the culture of the country is

_____

No. of speakers: _____

2) _____

They live in countries where English

may be used for _____

_____ , e.g., _____

No. of speakers: _____

(estimate by Prof. _____)

3) Learners of Eng. _____

They live in _____

They need English for _____

and _____ purposes

No. of speakers: _____

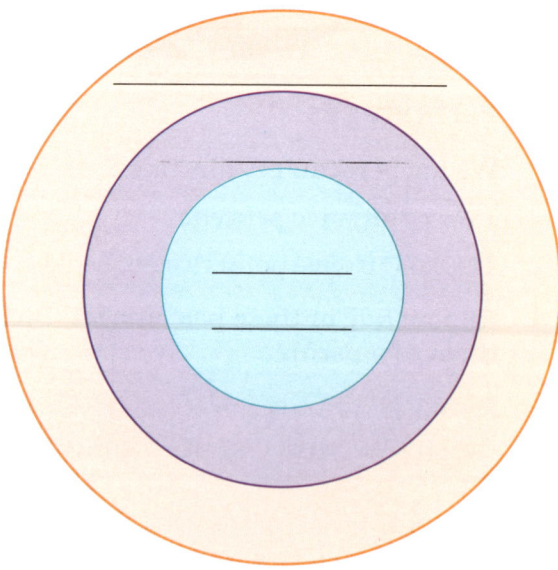

Three circles of English –
after _____, 19____

Discussion

3 Discuss these questions in small groups.

a) Which type of English speaker are you?

b) Which other languages are important now?

c) Which languages will be important in the future? Why?

Skills in Focus – reading and writing

Reading

1 Discuss these questions in groups.

a) What is 'software'? Give some examples.

b) What is 'automatic translation software'?

c) Is it possible to have such software (or a machine that translates)? What are the problems?

2 Read the advertisement for Easyword.

a) What problem does the writer describe?

b) What solution does the advertisement give?

c) What other things could you do in that situation?

d) How can you use the software? Describe the steps.

3 In groups, design a poster to advertise the *Easyword Translator*.

EASYWORD TRANSLATORS

THE PROBLEM

You have to send an urgent message to a company in Japan. It's very important for your business. You are very close to signing a big deal. But there's one problem: you can't speak or write a word of Japanese. What's more, you need to send the message in half an hour. What do you do?

You could try to find a translator and pay them to translate the message. You could make sure there was a Japanese speaker working in your company. Or you could even learn Japanese!

OUR SOLUTION

Fortunately, New Star Communications have a solution to your translation problems. It's called Easyword and it's our new automatic translation software. Cheap, fast and simple to use, Easyword will solve all your translation worries.

HOW DOES IT WORK?

It's easy! First, of course, you install the software. Then you simply type your message into the computer, select the language you need, in this case Japanese, and press a key. And that's it – in seconds you have an automatic translation into the language you want.

Easyword gives you a choice of eight different languages: English, French, Chinese, Arabic, Spanish, Italian, Turkish and, of course, Japanese. Is this science fiction? No, it's science fact! With our software you can translate documents and e-mail messages automatically. Trust us. It will change the way you do business … forever.

HOW CAN I GET MORE INFORMATION?

Complete the form below, visit our website or write directly to us at **Easyword, PO Box 3421, Singapore.**

PUT AN END TO YOUR LANGUAGE PROBLEMS!

Writing

4 Write a letter to Easyword about their advertisement. Ask for more information (brochures, prices, etc.). Ask if they have software for German translation.

5 Look at the notes below about the Japanese language. Rewrite them using the abbreviations in the Study Skills section (and your own abbreviations). Use headings and layout to make the notes clearer.

Japanese language – official language of Japan. Spoken by approximately 125 million inhabitants. Its vocabulary, sound system and grammar are very different to other languages. Vocabulary: three types of word – the first are native Japanese words, second are words borrowed in ancient times from Chinese, third (small but growing very rapidly) are words borrowed in modern times, for example, from English and other Asian languages. Sounds – Japanese open-sound system (that is to say, most syllables end in a vowel), also 'pitch' is very important in Japanese. Grammar – word order in English: subject/verb/object – word order in Japanese: verb is at the end of the sentence (that is to say, subject/object/verb).

Study Tip | Use abbreviations and headings in notes

Everyone has their own way of taking notes, but here are some more tips.

Abbreviations

Use abbreviations when you can. Here are some common examples:

=	–	equals
≠	–	does not equal
&	–	and
no.	–	number
imp.	–	important
v.	–	very
i.e.	–	that is to say
poss.	–	possibly
esp.	–	especially
∴	–	therefore
N.B.	–	note
p.	–	page
approx.	–	approximately
max.	–	maximum
min.	–	minimum

Headings

Use headings and subheadings to show when a new point begins. Underline or highlight the headings.

Types of English speaker:

1) *Native English speakers –*

   _____

2) *Second language speakers –*

   _____

3) *Foreign language learners –*

   _____

Vocabulary Review
Countries, nationalities and languages

1 Complete this table with words from the unit.

country	nationality	language
Turkey	Turkish	Turkish
United States	American	English
United Kingdom		

Task 1: Write six sentences using words from the table (two from each column).

For example:

I would love to visit Brazil.

My fiancé is Turkish.

Percentages and decimals

2 Practise pronouncing the percentages below.

55%   = fifty-five per cent

46.8%   = forty-six point eight per cent

0.5%   = nought point five per cent

19.19%   = nineteen point one nine per cent

Grammar Review

- **could/couldn't**

present	can	can't (cannot)
past	could	couldn't (could not)

Simon **could** swim quite well when he was young.

Mary **couldn't** speak a word of English last year.

Task 2: Write three sentences using *could* and *couldn't*.

- **Past time phrases**

last	year/month/week
six years/five minutes/ two days/a long time	ago
in	March/1998/the 20th century

There was an earthquake in Turkey **last year**

I don't know where Georgio is. He was here **a few minutes ago**.

In the 17th century the Philippines was a Spanish colony.

Language Review

- **Making requests**

Can/Could I (possibly) ... ?

Can/Could you (possibly) ... ?

- **Saying yes**

Yes, of course.

Certainly.

Sure.

OK.

- **Saying no**

I'm sorry. I ... .

I'm afraid I ... .

Task 3: Write a short dialogue like the one below.

Could you possibly turn that music down?

I'm afraid I can't hear you. I'm listening to some music.

Introduction

Discussion

1 It's the summer vacation at the New International University. The students are going home or having holidays.

Work in pairs. Match these sentences with pictures A–D.

"What's that building over there?" _____

"We'd like a double room, please." _____

"Would you like a window seat or an aisle seat?" _____

"This steak is delicious." _____

Vocabulary

2 Make a list of ten words (nouns, verbs and adjectives) to go with each of the four situations.

Listening

Listen to four short dialogues. What are the people doing? Write letters A–D.

booking a hotel room _____

sightseeing _____

ordering a meal _____

booking a flight _____

Reading

Read these postcards, letters and e-mails. Match them to the pictures on page 102.

A

Dear Yuki,

We are really enjoying our holiday in Australia. At the moment we are staying in Sydney. It's a great city. Yesterday we had a tour: we saw the opera house and we went on a boat trip around the harbour. You can see the harbour on this card. We walked all over the city. At the moment we're resting. My feet are hurting!

Love, Maria and Rosa

B

Felix,

Yesterday I saw Adel and Sami. We had a meal together in a restaurant. We talked about the business plan. They're writing a report and they'll send me a copy as soon as they've finished. I'm also waiting for a phone call from Bill. He's planning to join us. I'll be in touch when I have more news. We must keep this plan quiet. Don't tell anyone!

Regards,
Hassan

C

We're staying in the Hotel Paradiso at the moment. It's terrible. The rooms are small and not very clean. And the beds are hard and uncomfortable. Yesterday I saw a cockroach in the bathroom!

I'm writing this letter in the lounge. It's raining hard outside and the wind is blowing, so we have to stay in the hotel. I can't wait to come home!

Best wishes,
Lee

D

Hi! I hope you received the postcard I sent last week from Delhi. I'm writing this message on my new laptop. I'm on a plane and I'm flying to Colombo from Madras. I was in Madras for two days. I met an old friend of mine, Gulrez. He's studying at the University of Madras. We had a great time. The weather was very hot and humid. I hope it will be cooler in Colombo. I'll phone you in a couple of days.

Afzal

Sightseeing

Write the names of the following sights. Can you give a famous example of each one?

103

Language in Focus

Thinking about grammar
Present continuous

1 Look at the sentences and complete the table below.

a) We are really enjoying our holiday in Australia.

b) I am writing this message on my new laptop.

c) It is raining hard and the wind is blowing.

d) He is studying at the university in Madras.

e) They are writing a report about transport.

f) Are you staying at the Grand Hotel?

I		
You		
He/She/It		enjoying the vacation.
We		
They		

2 Find more present continuous verb forms in the texts on page 103. Underline the verbs.

3 Look at the pictures below. Describe what is happening and what the people are doing. Use the present continuous tense and these verbs: *to snow, to wait (for), to write, to study*.

A

Chantelle.

B

C

D *Raymond*

Thinking about grammar
Past simple – irregular forms

4 Look at the sentences and write the infinitives of the underlined verbs.

meet
a) Hari <u>met</u> Jack at the airport last week.

b) On Friday we <u>had</u> a meal in a restaurant.

c) I <u>saw</u> Mike about two weeks ago.

d) They <u>went</u> on a tour of the city yesterday.

5 Scan the texts on page 103 again and circle the irregular past forms.

Holiday vocabulary

6 Match the verbs and nouns by putting ticks (✓) in the table.

	a single/ double room	breakfast/ lunch/dinner	a taxi
book			
have			
order			
serve			

7 Complete the dialogue with vocabulary from the table above.

A: I'd like to ① _____, please.

B: Certainly. A single or a ② _____?

A: A single, please, for tonight.

B: That's fine.

A: What time do you ③ _____?

B: From 6.30 to 10. Would you like to ④ _____ in your room?

A: Yes, please, at 6.30. I have to leave early. Could you possibly ⑤ _____ for me?

B: Yes, of course. I'll ask the porter. At what time?

A: Er … 7.30, I think.

Booking a flight

8 Listen and complete the telephone conversation with phrases from the box below.

> Business class   does it arrive
> at 17.35   I'd like to book   we must be
> the return fare   on the 26th   It departs
> How many   How much
> at 13.55   That flight's full

A: Hello, Flight Reservations.

B: Hello. ① _____ a flight to Cairo.

A: Certainly. ② _____ people is it for?

B: Two.

A: And when would you like to fly?

B: On the 18th of January, and I want to

return ③ _____ .

A: Let me check … Yes, there's a flight at

14.00 hours on the 18th. Flight AK967.

B: When ④ _____ in Cairo?

A: ⑤ _____ .

B: And what about the return flight?

A: ⑥ _____ at 08.45 and arrives in

Muscat at 10.20.

B: Fine.

A: Oh, just a minute. ⑦ _____ .

B: But ⑧ _____ in Muscat on the 26th.

A: There's a flight ⑨ _____ , arriving in

Muscat at 16.25. Shall I book that for you?

B: Yes, that's fine. ⑩ _____ does it cost?

A: ⑪ _____ or economy?

B: Economy.

A: ⑫ _____ is 240 riyals.

B: That's great.

Role play

9 **Student A:** You want to travel to Cairo from Athens. You must be in Cairo before 5 o'clock in the afternoon. Book a flight with the travel agent. You want an Economy Class ticket.

Student B: You are the travel agent. Find out what the customer needs and arrange a flight. Use the flight information in the table below. Fill in the booking form.

flight no.	depart Athens	arrive Cairo	price: economy return ($US)
SU176	09.45	12.30	350
ME89	11.05	14.50	325
QA546	13.35	16.15	375

BOOKING FORM

Name _____

Flight no. _____

From _____ to _____

Departure time _____ arrival _____

Class _____ Price _____

Thinking about grammar
must/have to

- I **must be** in Cairo by 5. It is very important.
- I **have to be** in Cairo by 5.

10 **Find two more examples of *must* and *have/has* to in the texts on page 103 and add them to the table.**

subject	must/have (has) to	main verb	
Sami	must	work	hard.
My sister	has to	go	to the hospital.
You	must	see	that film.

Skills in Focus – listening and speaking

Listening

1 Mary is on her mobile phone. Where is she? Listen and choose picture A, B, C or D.

2 Listen again and say if these statements are true or false. Correct the false statements.

a) Mary is on holiday with her sister.

b) The weather is very hot today.

c) They saw the Topkapi Palace yesterday.

d) They went on a boat trip yesterday.

e) They are going to the Ataturk Museum tomorrow.

f) They had fish for dinner last night.

g) They had dinner in the hotel.

Presentation

3 Work in small groups. You are planning a tour for visitors. Make a list of the top six sights in a city or region you know.

> *Sights you must see*
>
> *1. the cathedral*

4 Imagine your class is a tour group. Prepare a short talk about the place you chose. Tell the group about the six sights they must see and explain why.

Role play

5 Work in pairs. You are on holiday and you are on the phone describing the scene from your hotel window to your friend.

Student A: Describe the scene below and the people in it using verbs in the present continuous form (e.g., *selling, sitting*).

Student B: Turn to page 108.

Skills in Focus – reading and writing

Reading

1 Use the hotel brochure and the room rates to find out the following information. Discuss with a partner.

a) You are arriving by train with a suitcase. Can you walk to the hotel from the station?

b) You want to eat in the hotel when you arrive. It will be about 11.00 in the evening. Is it possible?

c) You would like a room with an en-suite bathroom and a TV. Are you sure you will have one?

d) You want to stay in February. How much will you pay for a double room with a bathroom for two nights?

Room rates per night (in euros):

	Oct–March	April–Sept
Single room	45	52
Single room (en suite)	50	57
Double room	55	65
Double room (en suite)	60	70

All prices include continental breakfast.

Hotel Paradiso

Welcome to Hotel Paradiso. It's a lovely place and once you check in you won't want to leave! We offer you comfort and cleanliness at a very reasonable rate.

Location The hotel is situated right opposite the main bus station and just half a kilometre from the railway station. It is also convenient for those guests arriving by car, as a motorway passes just behind the hotel. There is a car park at the end of the road. From the hotel you can walk to the city centre in just 15 minutes. The National Museum and the Grand Palace are just 200 metres away.

Facilities The hotel has six floors. We will soon be installing a lift. There are 25 single and double rooms and a luxury suite on the top floor. Many rooms have en-suite bathrooms and satellite TV. There is a restaurant on the first floor serving delicious international food, prepared by our own chef. On the top floor there is a bar and a small cafe where you can enjoy the fine views of the bus station and the motorway. There is also a comfortable lounge next to the lobby where you can relax after sightseeing.

Meals Breakfast is served in our attractive dining room from 7.00 to 8.30. Lunch is from 12.30 p.m. to 3.00 p.m. Dinner is served from 6.30 p.m. to 9.30 p.m. (last orders at 9.00 p.m.). There is also room service available from 6.30 in the morning to midnight.

Information For further information and details of our reasonable rates, please contact our reception desk on **987 555481**.

Hotel Paradiso ...
It could be heaven!

2 Work with a partner to find some advantages and disadvantages of staying in the hotel. Would you choose to stay there?

Writing

1 Read the texts on page 103 again. Write a postcard, e-mail or letter to friends or family. Describe:

a) where you are writing from.

b) the weather and the hotel you are staying in.

c) what you did yesterday.

Role play (page 107)

Student B: Listen to your partner's description. Now describe the scene below and the people in it using verbs in the present continuous form (e.g., *having a picnic*, *sailing*).

Study Tip — Use different sources of information – including your computer!

Surf the Internet to get the information you want. Get information about:

- your subject area.
- learning English.

Make a note of all the useful sites. Also use CD-ROMs. Find out what CD-ROMs are available for language study and for your subject.

Tip: Try Dave Sperling's ESL Café:
http://www.eslcafe.com

1 What other sources of information are there? Are there special sources for your subject? Work in pairs and make a list.

2 Choose one of the topics below (choose something that is new to you). Find information about it, using as many different sources as you can. Take notes and then write a paragraph on the subject.

henna   baseball   Gracelands
Lake Baikal   prawns   webcams
booking flights on-line   cloning
malaria   flamenco music

Vocabulary Review
Travel and tourism

1 Put these words connected with hotels into groups (e.g., *meals*, *staff*). Add any other words you know to your groups.

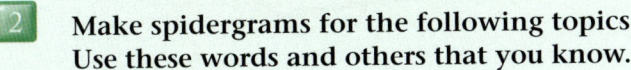

> waiter lunch single bathroom
> to order breakfast lounge
> to check in dining room porter
> to serve lobby cafe double
> receptionist to book dinner bar
> en suite to reserve

2 Make spidergrams for the following topics. Use these words and others that you know.

a) **air travel**: *check in, luggage, aisle seat, window seat*

b) **sightseeing**: *to go on a tour, to go on a boat trip, statue, museum, art gallery*

Grammar Review
- ### Present continuous

We use this tense for actions that are happening at the moment of speaking, for example:

> It's raining.

> Two men are walking along the street.

or for temporary situations:

> We are staying in a lovely hotel in Hong Kong.

> I'm studying Engineering at the Millennium University.

Task 1: Write five sentences about what you are doing/what someone you know is doing at the moment.

- ### must/have to

Must is a modal, like *can* and *could*. It comes before the main verb.

> Juan **must** work hard. He has an exam next week.

> All passengers **must** show their boarding cards.

The meaning of *have/has to* is similar to *must*.

> We **have to** write an essay by tomorrow.

> I **have to** write a letter.

> Beth **has to** see the Dean today.

> You **have to** phone him! It's very important.

Task 2: Make a list of the things you must/have to do in the next week.

- ### Past simple – irregular forms

verb	past simple
go	went
have	had
meet	met
see	saw

Task 3: Add more verbs with irregular past simple forms to the table from the unit and your own knowledge.

Language Review
- ### Booking a flight

I'd like to book a flight to …

How much does it cost?

When does that flight leave/depart/arrive?

It leaves/departs/arrives at …

Would you like an aisle seat or a window seat?

Task 4: Write a dialogue between a travel agent and a customer.

Introduction

Discussion

1 **Look at these pictures.**

a) What are the students doing?

b) What do you think of these ways of studying? Discuss the advantages and disadvantages.

Listening

2 Rosa is talking to one of her lecturers, Mrs Russell. They are discussing the best way to study. What advice does Mrs Russell give? Make notes below.

You should ... _____

_____

_____

_____

You shouldn't ... _____

_____

_____

_____

Reading

3 **Read these ideas for improving your memory. Do you agree with them? Discuss in your group.**

a) It is easier to remember information when it is organised.

b) You should try to use mental pictures to help you remember.

c) You should take breaks when you are trying to learn something.

d) You can't remember information if you don't concentrate in the first place.

4 **Match the ideas above with paragraphs A–D of the article below.**

Can't remember?

Read through this list of words slowly. Then cover them up and try to remember as many as you can. Write them on a piece of paper.

> suitcase   breakfast   hand   tree
> bag   happiness   lunch   meaning
> dinner   backpack   love   time
> staple   Amazon   preposterous   meal
> modern   teacher   building
> briefcase   handbag

Compare your list with a friend. Which words did you remember? Which words did you forget? Why do you think you could remember some words and not others?

A This graph shows how well people can remember what they are studying.

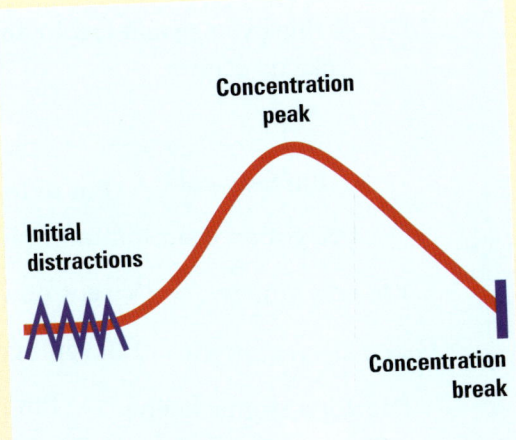

Most people find it difficult to concentrate for more than 20 minutes.

B If you get a list of words, you should try to put them into groups. It is easier to remember words in this way. For example, in the list, *breakfast*, *lunch* and *dinner* were probably easy to remember because they are all meals. Also *suitcase, bag, backpack*, etc., are easier to remember if you see that they are all different kinds of luggage.

C Researchers say that the main reason we do not remember things is because we are not paying attention in the first place. We usually forget 70% of what we learn in 24 hours. In order to remember something, we have to want to remember it. This means we ought to make a special effort to move the information from our short-term to our long-term memory.

D The strongest part of our memory is the visual memory. If, for example, you associate a picture of a lot of trees with the word *forest*, then it will be easier to remember. Similarly, an image of a briefcase will help you to remember the word *briefcase*. Words like *happiness* and *meaning* are difficult to visualise. Because of this, they are more difficult to remember.

Language in Focus

Thinking about grammar
should, ought to
(should not, ought not to)

1 Put these words in the correct order to make sentences.

a) study/a/make/students/plan/should

b) plenty/ought to/exercise/you/get/of

c) take/a lot of/should/breaks/you

d) harder/ought to/much/Rosa/work

e) tired/are/study/shouldn't/when/you/you

2 Add the main verbs from Exercise 1 to the table.

subject	modal verb	main verb
I, You, He, She, It, We, They	should	
	ought to	
	can	
	could	
	must	
	have to	

Giving advice

3 Give advice to these people. Write sentences with *should*, *shouldn't* or *ought to*. For example:

"You shouldn't drive with one hand."

"You should drive more carefully."

A

B

C

D

4 Work with a partner. Choose problems from the list and practise giving advice. Use *should*, *shouldn't* or *ought to*.

A: What's the matter?

B: I've got a headache.

A: I think you should (ought to) go home and take an aspirin.

I'm very cold.   I'm in love.

I've got an examination tomorrow.

I'm very thirsty.   I've got nowhere to live.

I can't sleep at night.   I haven't got any money.

I've got a stomachache.   I'm feeling sad.

I'm homesick.   I've got a job interview.

My car's broken down.

Listening

5 Felipe is trying to read. His brother, Manuel, wants to talk. Listen to their conversation and complete it with the questions below.

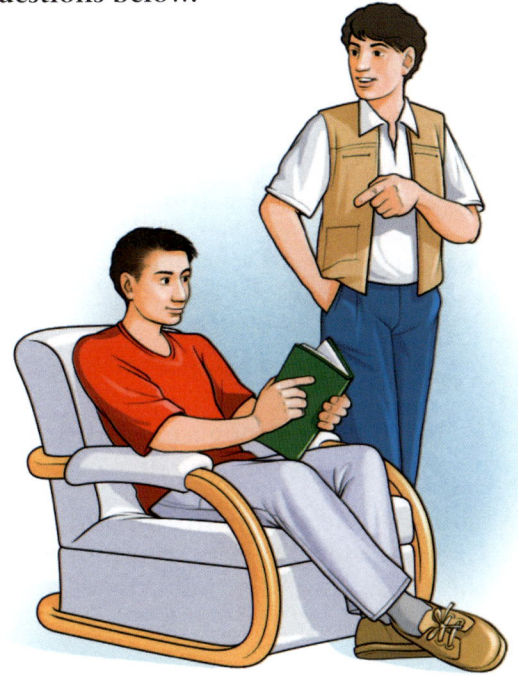

What are you reading?

Are you enjoying it?

I know it's a book, but what's it about?

What are you doing, Felipe?

Why are you studying psychology?

Manuel: ① _____?

Felipe: I'm reading.

Manuel: ② _____?

Felipe: A book.

Manuel: ③ _____?

Felipe: It's about psychology.

Manuel: ④ _____?

Felipe: I'm not studying psychology. I'm just interested in it.

Manuel: ⑤ _____?

Felipe: Yes, I was, until you started asking questions. Go away.

Thinking about grammar
Present continuous – questions and negatives

6 Underline the questions and negative forms of the present continuous in this dialogue. Then complete the tables.

A: Hi, Barbara. Are you busy?

B: No, I'm not doing very much – just reading a magazine. What are you doing?

A: Well, I'm watching TV and Andy's doing his homework.

B: What about Joe? Is he studying for his exam?

A: No! He isn't studying. He's playing football in the street!

I	am	not	studying.
You, We, They	are		
He, She, It	____		

Am	I		waiting?
____	you, we, they		
Is	he, she, it		

7 Samia is at a job interview. Complete the dialogue (I = interviewer, S = Samia). Put the verbs in brackets in the present continuous form.

I: ① ____ you _____ at the moment? (work)

S: No, I ② ____. (not work) I ③ ____. (study)

I: Oh? Where?

S: At the New International University.

I: Which subjects ④ ____ you _____? (take)

S: French, English and Business Studies.

I: I see. Why ⑤ _____ you _____ for this job? (apply)

S: I need some business experience. So I ⑥ _____ a part-time job. (look for)

I: And why this company? We need experienced people here. We ⑦ _____ students. (not recruit)

S: My uncle works here. He's the managing director!

113

Skills in Focus – listening and speaking

 1 Many people say that motivation is the key to success. What motivates you to study? Read these comments by students and discuss them in groups.

> I like my subject and I want to learn everything about it.

> I need good qualifications if I want to be a successful and respected person.

> My lecturer is very enthusiastic – he makes me want to learn more about the subject.

> I like working with other students.

> I want a good job with lots of money, so I need to study hard.

> I like to think that I am improving myself by learning new skills.

Listening

 2 Listen to the psychologist, Dr Kim, talking about motivation. Complete the notes below.

MOTIVATION

<u>Success in studying</u> — depends on:
- intelligence
- _____
- _____
- quality of instruction (i.e., teachers, lecturers)
- and (most important) _____

<u>Motivation</u> — causes people to _____ _____, to move

<u>Two types of motivation:</u>

1. _____

2. intrinsic (inside)

3 Now look at the comments in Exercise 1 again. Which are examples of intrinsic motivation?

Debate

4 Read this short text and discuss the following question in groups.

SCIENCE NEWS
Advances in research into DNA mean that soon scientists may have the technology they need to improve the intelligence of Man. It may be possible for couples to have more intelligent babies.

Q: Is it right or wrong for scientists to try to make people more intelligent?

Think of the arguments for and against. Give the views of your group to the rest of the class.

1. _____ — studying in order to get something, e.g., to get a good job/money

   — _____

   — to master a subject/skill

   Problem — rewards are _____

2. <u>Intrinsic</u> — comes from studying, e.g.,

   — pleasure of learning something new

   — _____

   _____

   — motivation of teachers and lecturers

Good thing — the reward is _____

— you don't have to _____

<u>Conclusion</u>   Intrinsic factors are _____ — because they _____

Skills in Focus – reading and writing

Reading

1 **Read the article about Supermouse quickly.**

a) Put the paragraphs in the right order. Check your answer with a partner.

b) Think of a different title for the text. Compare your title with other students.

2 **Read the article again and decide if these statements are true (T) or false (F). Correct the false statements.**

a) Doogie eats and sleeps like an ordinary mouse. ( )

b) Doogie is more intelligent than the other mice in the laboratory. ( )

c) Doogie's memory is the same as other mice. ( )

d) Scientists made changes to Doogie's DNA. ( )

e) Scientists may also improve Man's intelligence. ( )

f) Most scientists think it is important to try to produce 'superbabies'. ( )

3 **Complete the table with words from the text.**

adjective	noun
intelligent	
possible	
	science
interesting	
	fantasy

SUPERMOUSE

A) Although the experiments on Doogie are causing a lot of interest in the scientific world, most scientists think that there are more important uses of the technology than trying to produce 'superbabies'. For example, people with memory problems or diseases such as Alzheimer's could be helped by this research. It has very interesting possibilities.

B) It is clear that Doogie's brain is better than the brain of a normal mouse. But this is not an accident. Scientists at the university changed the DNA of the mouse. This changed the reactions inside the brain of the mouse and made it more intelligent. It also gave Doogie a better memory than his slower cousins.

C) Doogie looks like an ordinary mouse. He is brown and furry. He lives in a laboratory in the Molecular Biology Department of Princedown University in the USA. Just like the other mice in the laboratory, he eats, sleeps and climbs the bars in his cage.

D) This story seems like a fantasy. But it could be even more fantastic. There are all kinds of possible uses for this technology. For example, scientists say that they could probably improve the intelligence and memory of Man. Parents might try to improve the intelligence of their children.

E) But, in fact, Doogie is not ordinary at all. When the researchers give the mouse tasks to do, he leaves all the other mice far behind. He finishes the tasks more quickly than the others. He also learns faster and he remembers things for longer than the other mice. Doogie cannot actually fly, but in every other way he really is a 'supermouse'.

Reading and writing

4 Read these three letters and e-mails from students at the New International University. They all have problems. What are they?

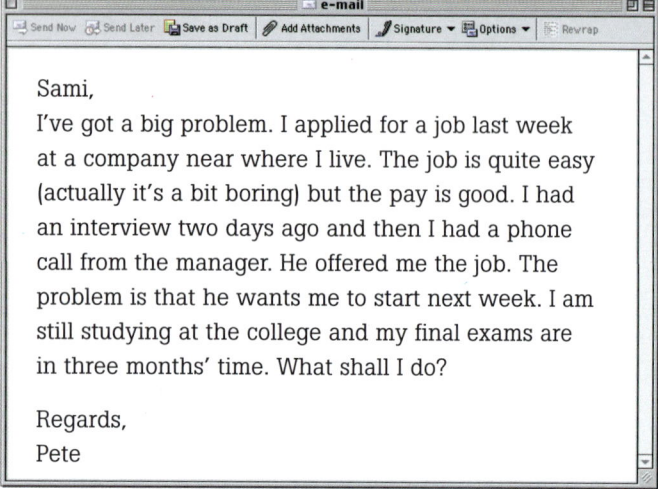

Sami,

I've got a big problem. I applied for a job last week at a company near where I live. The job is quite easy (actually it's a bit boring) but the pay is good. I had an interview two days ago and then I had a phone call from the manager. He offered me the job. The problem is that he wants me to start next week. I am still studying at the college and my final exams are in three months' time. What shall I do?

Regards,
Pete

Dear Sue,

How are you? I hope you are well. Are you enjoying your new job?

Things are not so good here at the college. I am not feeling well at all. I can't sleep and I can't study. I find it so difficult to concentrate. I am tired all the time. Yesterday I fell asleep in a lecture! What do you think is wrong? What should I do?

I'm looking forward to hearing from you.
Love and best wishes,

Roxanne

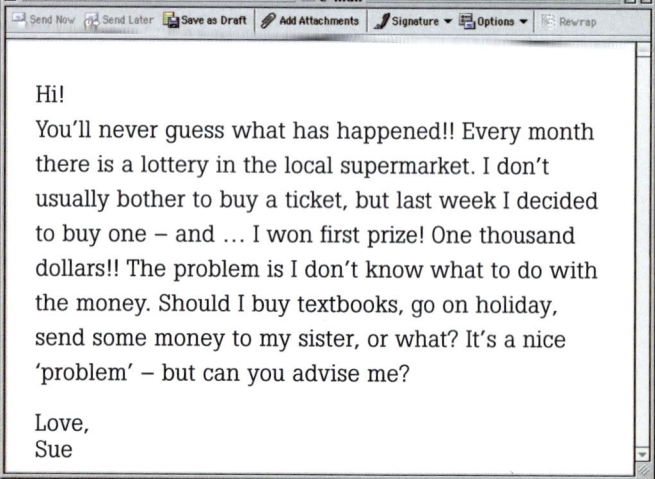

Hi!

You'll never guess what has happened!! Every month there is a lottery in the local supermarket. I don't usually bother to buy a ticket, but last week I decided to buy one – and … I won first prize! One thousand dollars!! The problem is I don't know what to do with the money. Should I buy textbooks, go on holiday, send some money to my sister, or what? It's a nice 'problem' – but can you advise me?

Love,
Sue

5 Choose one of the letters and e-mails above. Write a reply, giving advice.

Study Skills and Review

Study Tip | **Make a memory map**

Make your notes visual. This makes them easier to remember. A memory map looks like this. It is a mixture of words, symbols, pictures and colours.

Remember: Your brain likes pictures and maps!

1 Listen to Dr Kim's lecture again and make your own memory map.

2 Read the article about Supermouse again. Make a memory map of the key information.

Vocabulary Review

Learning

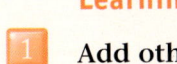 Add other verbs related to learning to this spidergram.

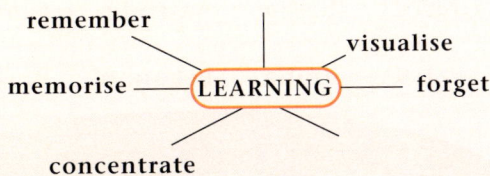

Opposites

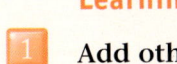 Make pairs of opposite adjectives with the words below.

> easy   late   less   long
> difficult   fast   more   early
> slow   short   ordinary   special
> interesting   boring

Verbs and nouns

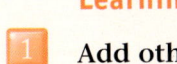 Match the verbs on the left with the nouns on the right.

apply for	
make	
look for	some notes
take	a job
accept	

Task 1: Write two sentences using the verb and noun combinations above.

Grammar Review

- **Present continuous – questions and negatives**

I	am	not studying.
You, We, They	are	
He, She, It	is	

Am	I	waiting?
Are	you, we, they	
Is	he, she, it	

I'**m not working** at the moment. I'**m looking** for a job.

"**Is** Peter **sending** an e-mail?"

"No. He'**s surfing** the Internet."

Task 2: What are you doing at college or work at the moment? Write a dialogue between yourself and a friend. Use the present continuous tense to describe your current projects.

- **Modals**

Should and *ought to* are modal verbs. They come before the main verb.

You **should** make notes.

He **ought to** say sorry.

They **shouldn't** be smoking in here.

Language Review

- **Asking for and giving advice**

What should I do?

(I think) you should/ought to …

I don't think you should/ought to …

You shouldn't …

I think you should buy a new car.

We don't think you should take this job.

You ought to stay at college for another year.

Task 3: Write five sentences about people you know, giving advice. Use *should, ought to* and *shouldn't*.

For example:

My brother shouldn't spend so much time watching TV.

Samia ought to get up earlier in the morning.

Introduction

Discussion

1 Look at the pictures of 12 famous people. In groups, match the pictures with these names:

Yuri Gargarin, Omar Sharif, Plato, Pelé, Amitabh Bachchan, Muhammad Ali, Nicole Kidman, Karl Marx, Marie Curie, Kofi Annan, Fairuz, Ataturk.

2 Now match the people with their countries and the field they became famous in.

Poland   Egypt   Turkey   Ghana

Greece   Russia   Australia   Germany

USA   India   Lebanon   Brazil

films   politics   science

philosophy   singing   sport

3 Use these adjectives (and others) to describe some of the people in the list:

important   beautiful   arrogant
handsome   kind   brave   intelligent
attractive   skilful   dangerous
wonderful   great   interesting

Examples:

I think ... is very intelligent.

I think ... was a wonderful actor.

... has an interesting face.

4 Which of the 12 people are (or were) the most important for the world? Discuss with your group and choose three. Explain your choice to the class.

Listening

5 Listen to two friends talking about two of the people in the list. Who are they?

A: _____

B: _____

Reading

6 Read about Marie Curie and Yuri Gagarin. Complete the notes in the table.

name		
born (date) (place)		
lived		
profession		
studied		
died (date)		

Narrating

When we tell a story or write about someone's life, we use time phrases. Look at these examples from the life of Marie Curie.

… on May 15th, 1867.

At the age of …

Two years later …

In 1894 …

… the following year.

7 Read the text about Yuri Gagarin again. Circle the time phrases.

Marie Curie

Marie Sklodowska was born in Poland on May 15th, 1867. Her father was a teacher of Physics. At the age of 22, Marie went to Paris and studied Physics at the Sorbonne. Two years later she passed her examinations in Physics with the highest marks of all the students.

In 1894, she met Pierre Curie, also a famous scientist, and they got married the following year.

Marie was interested in radiation and invented the term 'radioactive'. Pierre joined his wife in the study of radiation, and in 1903 they received the Nobel Prize for Physics. Marie was the first woman to receive a Nobel prize. In 1911, Marie Curie received a second Nobel prize. This time it was for Chemistry. Marie Curie died in 1934. She was one of the greatest scientists of the 20th century.

Yuri Gagarin

Yuri Gagarin was a famous Russian cosmonaut. He was the first person to fly in space. In 1961 he made one orbit of the Earth abroad the spacecraft, *Vostok 1*.

Gagarin was born on March 9th, 1934, in Smolensk in the former Soviet Union. At the age of 16 he moved to Saratov, to the southeast of Moscow, where he went to technical school. While he was there, he joined a flying club and learned to fly aeroplanes. In 1955, he joined the air force and studied at the Soviet air force cadet training school in Chkalov. After two years, he graduated with high distinction.

After his historic flight in 1961, Gagarin became a national hero and travelled all over the world. However, he died tragically in March 1968, at the age of only 33. He was killed in a plane crash.

Language in Focus

Thinking about grammar
was/were born

1 Complete the sentences with **was** or **were**.

a) Lee _____ born in Hong Kong in 1984.

b) Where _____ Rosa born – in Italy or France?

c) When _____ you born, Sarah?

d) I _____ born in Manila in 1985.

e) Hassan and Ahmed _____ born in Egypt.

2 Discuss these questions with a partner.

a) When was Yuri Gagarin born?

b) Where was Marie Curie born?

c) When were you born?

d) Where were you born?

Thinking about grammar
Past simple – regular forms

3 Underline the verbs in these sentences.

a) Marie went to Paris and studied Physics at the Sorbonne.

b) In 1911, Marie Curie received a second Nobel prize.

c) Marie Curie died in 1934.

d) She was one of the greatest scientists of the 20th century.

4 How many regular and irregular verbs are there in Exercise 3?

Note:

- Regular past verbs add **-ed**, **-d** or **-ied**.

  pass – pass**ed**
  die – di**ed**
  marry – marr**ied** ('y' changes to 'i')

- The ending is the same for all forms.

5 Read about Yuri Gagarin again. Underline all the past forms and decide if they are regular or irregular.

6 Complete these sentences with the correct past simple form.

a) Ten years ago we _____ (live) in Tokyo.

b) Last summer Ali and his family _____ (go) to Beirut for a holiday.

c) Princess Diana _____ (die) in Paris.

d) Many years ago I _____ (meet) the King of Sweden.

e) My younger sister _____ (get) married in March last year.

f) My father _____ (work) in a factory near Ankara from 1993 to 2001.

g) I _____ (become) very interested in aeroplanes when I _____ (be) a young boy.

h) Fatima _____ (have) a difficult time at university, but she _____ (pass) the examination in the end.

7 Listen to the endings of these past forms. Write them in the correct column of the table.

invented	worked	joined	returned
	asked	wanted	

/t/	/d/	/ɪd/
passed	lived	decided

Tag questions

Tags are a way of asking questions or asking for agreement. For example:

- He's a great actor, isn't he?

- She was beautiful, wasn't she?

- You remember me, don't you?

8 Complete these questions with tags.

a) You are from Beijing, _____?

b) Those cakes were terrible, _____?

c) George likes action films, _____?

Thinking about grammar
Comparatives and superlatives

A He's a **great** singer.

He's **greater than** Pavarotti.

He's **the greatest** singer in the world.

B She's a **beautiful** model.

She's **more beautiful** than Kate Moss.

She's **the most beautiful** model in the world.

9 Do these adjectives follow pattern A or pattern B? Write A or B below.

attractive	_____	brave	_____
cold	_____	interesting	_____
famous	_____	large	_____

10 Now write sentences like the examples above for each adjective.

11 **Good** and **bad** follow pattern A, but they have irregular forms. What are they?

Listening

12 Listen to Gita (G) and Meryl (M) talking about film stars. Who are their favourite actresses and actors?

G: What are you reading, Meryl?

M: Only a film magazine. Look at this

picture. She's beautiful, ① _____ ?

G: Who is it?

M: That's Sophia Loren, of course. She's

② _____ actress in the world – and the best.

G: She was, perhaps. I think Julia Roberts is

more beautiful than her. And a

③ _____ actress. You remember the

film *Notting Hill*, ④ _____ ?

M: No, I didn't see that. What about actors?

Who's ⑤ _____ , do you think?

G: Well, the Indian actor Amitabh Bachchan

is one of my ⑥ _____ , but I think

Omar Sharif is probably the best. He was

such a great actor, ⑦ _____ ?

M: No! I don't agree. He was very handsome,

and a good actor, but he wasn't great.

G: So who do you think is ⑧ _____ , then?

M: Tom Cruise.

G: Oh, no! He's probably ⑨ _____ . He's

always in those stupid action films. Did

you see *Mission Impossible*? It was terrible.

M: Yes, I ⑩ _____ it and I liked it.

G: Meryl, I think we'll have to agree to

disagree!

Past simple: questions and negatives

A: **Did** Hector **study** in Madrid?

B: No, he **studied** in Miami.

C: Where **did** you **buy** that beautiful dress?

D: I **didn't buy** it. Susie **bought** it. It was a gift!

E: Lee **didn't like** that film. **Did** you?

F: Yes, I **loved** it.

Now read the dialogue between Meryl and Gita again. Which verb appears in all three forms of the past simple (positive, negative and interrogative)?

121

Skills in Focus – listening and speaking

Speaking

1 Work in groups. Give Oscars in the following categories. Choose the best (and the worst) candidates for this year. Add other categories.

actor	actress
film	novel
popular singer	sportsman/woman
TV show	

2 Explain your group's choices to the rest of the class.

Listening

3 Who was Pelé? What do you know about his life? Discuss with a partner.

4 Listen to a radio programme about Pelé. Complete the notes below.

- Real name: _____ do Nascimento.

- Born (date) 1940   (place) _____

- 1st club _____ FC. Joined in _____.

- In 1962 _____.

- In 1970 he scored his _____ goal.

- Brazil won the World Cup with Pelé in _____, _____, and _____.

- In 1974 he _____. But then, from 1975 to 1977, he played for a team in _____.

- After 1977 he became _____ _____.

Research and speaking

5 Choose one of the famous people below. Find information about them using books, encyclopaedias, magazines, CD-ROMs and the Internet. Make notes like the ones about Pelé.

Ghandi

Cleopatra

Lenin

Christopher Columbus

Mao Zedong

Princess Diana

Nelson Mandela

Lee Kuan Yew

6 Prepare and give a five-minute presentation on the person you chose.

Make sure your talk has:

- an introduction (what you want to say);

- a main body (the talk);

- a closing (summarise what you said).

Skills in Focus – reading and writing

Reading

 Discuss these questions in groups.

a) Why do people want to be famous?

b) Would you like to be famous?

c) What are the advantages and disadvantages of fame?

d) Look at the title of the text. What do you think it means?

e) What is *The Guinness Book of World Records*?

 Read the article below and find the following information.

a) Who was Andy Warhol and what is 'pop art'?

b) Why did these people become famous: Gordon Cates, Chester Cable, Charlene Leatherman?

c) Why do people move to places such as Hollywood, Mumbai or London?

d) What kind of people are 'famous for being famous'?

e) What is the meaning of the title?

famous for fifteen minutes

An American pop artist, Andy Warhol, once said that in the future everyone would be 'world famous for 15 minutes'. Warhol, who died in 1987, was interested in the growth of the modern media in the 20th century. He liked to use images from the media and popular culture, such as pictures of soup cans and film stars like Marilyn Monroe, for his works of art. He thought that the rapid growth of the media was changing the world.

Some people, of course, will do absolutely anything to be famous. In 1999, Gordon Cates of Florida, USA, achieved fame by kissing the most snakes consecutively (a total of 11 poisonous cobras).

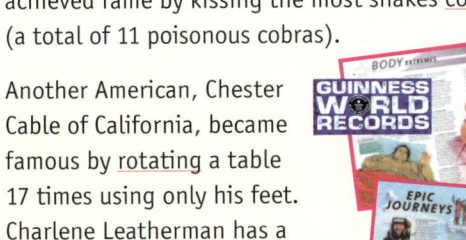

Another American, Chester Cable of California, became famous by rotating a table 17 times using only his feet. Charlene Leatherman has a collection of 793 dragons, the largest in the world. As a result of this unusual achievement, her name, along with those of thousands of other record-breakers, appears in *The Guinness Book of World Records*.

Aside from such strange ways of getting in the public eye, many people dream of achieving fame by becoming film stars or singers. Even though the chances of success are very small, thousands of young people move to places such as Hollywood, Mumbai or London every year to try to become successful actors, models or musicians.

Other people aim for fame by appearing on television 'reality' shows or by mixing with the rich and famous. These people, who have no real talent themselves, are often described as 'famous for being famous'.

What is the reason for this obsession with fame? It is partly, as Warhol said, because of the huge growth of the media around the world. Nowadays, almost everyone has access to television, films, newpapers and the Internet.

The obsession comes about mainly because people feel that their own lives are dull. We are fascinated by the lives of others – especially entertainers, politicians and royalty. We need to know what famous people are doing – or better still, to be famous ourselves, even if it is only for 15 minutes!

Writing

3 Interview your partner about his or her life. Use questions like the ones below and the time phrases on page 119.

When were you born?

Where did you go to school?

Tell me about ...

When was that?

How long did you ... ?

Write a paragraph about your partner as a biography in the past simple.

4 Write a biography of either:

a) the person you researched on page 122, using your notes,

or

b) a person you know and admire.

Mother Teresa

David Beckham

Study Skills and Review

Study Tip | Keep your reader interested!

When you write about a person's life, there is a danger that you will use the same sentence structure again and again.

Gagarin was born in 1934.

Gagarin graduated in 1951.

Gagarin went to industrial college.

Gagarin studied to be a pilot while he was at industrial college.

- You can make your writing more interesting by changing the person's name to the pronoun sometimes:

Gagarin was born in 1934.

He graduated in 1951.

He went on to industrial college.

Gagarin studied to be a pilot while he was at industrial college.

- You can improve your writing more by using *and* and *but* to link sentences that are connected. When you use these conjunctions, you don't need a noun or pronoun.

Gagarin was born in 1934 and graduated in 1951. He went on to industrial college and studied to be a pilot while he was there.

Write 10 sentences about a famous person from your country. Join some of the sentences with *and* or *but* to make two or three paragraphs.

Vocabulary Review

Describing a person

1 Copy this spidergram and add adjectives.

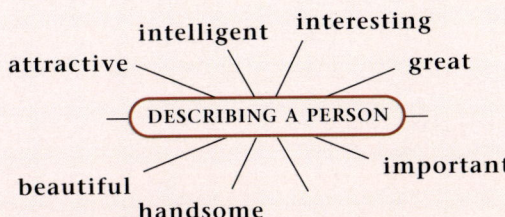

Telling the story of someone's life

2 Make a note of these verbs. Give an example of each in a sentence. Add other verbs you know: *to be born, to live, to study, to work, to die, to marry (to get married), to invent, to join, to return.*

3 **Professions**

Make a spidergram using these jobs and professions: *actor, politician, singer, scientist, writer, artist, teacher.* Add any other jobs that you know.

Grammar Review

● **Past simple – regular verbs**

We add *–ed, -d* or *-ied* to regular verbs to make the past tense.

I, You, He, She, It, We, They	work**ed** stud**ied** live**d**	in Beijing.

● **Past simple – irregular verbs**

Task 1: Complete the table.

irregular verb	past form
be	was/were
catch	_____
_____	drove
_____	got
have	_____
meet	_____
_____	saw
_____	spent
take	_____
write	_____

● **Comparatives and superlatives**

Short adjectives (regular)

Venezuela is **smaller than** Brazil.

Jupiter is **the largest** planet in the solar system.

Spelling note: big – bigger – biggest
hot – hotter – hottest
heavy – heavier – heaviest

Short adjectives (irregular)

adjective	comparative	superlative
good	better (than)	the best
bad	worse (than)	the worst

The weather is **better** this week **than** last week.

That's **the worst** lecture I've been to!

Long adjectives

Summer is **more beautiful than** winter in my country.

Tomorrow's exam is **the most important** of all!

Task 2: Choose three places you know. Write five sentences to compare them, using the superlative form of adjectives.

Introduction

Discussion

1. What are your plans for the end of your course of study? Discuss in small groups.

Listening

2. It's the end of the semester at the New International University. Some of the students are having a graduation party. Listen to five people talking about their plans for the future and complete the table.

name	future plans
Farida	1.
	2.
Lee	1.
	2.
Hassan	1.
	2.
Rosa	1.
	2.
Sarah	1.
	2.

Reading

3 Read these letters, notes and e-mails. Match the five speakers from the listening section with their messages.

A

Dear Monica,

This is just a note to say goodbye. I didn't see you at the party earlier and I am leaving tomorrow morning. As you know, I'm doing a course in London this summer and then I hope to get a job in Madrid – in an insurance company. I would like to see you again. Do come and visit me in Madrid – if I get my job! Good luck with your studies.

Lots of love,

D

Hello!

This is probably the last postcard I'll send you from Alumnia. I'm leaving in a couple of weeks. I'm going to spend a few days in Sydney and I hope to be with you in Brisbane by the end of the month. How's the weather? Did you book my diving course?

See you soon!

B

Hi Frank!

Just a note to let you know I'm arriving in Hong Kong on the 22nd. I've got to start work at the beginning of next month. Everything is fixed with the bank. I can't wait to start. Did you speak to Mo? I hope all the arrangements for the wedding are going well. I'll e-mail you again tomorrow.

Best wishes,

E

Dear Jo,

I'm going to be in the States in three weeks' time. I'm flying to Singapore first, then Tokyo and then San Francisco. I'd like to come and see you in LA. Are you going to be at home then?

My course here has finished and yesterday we had a graduation party. I'm not sure of my future plans. I want to travel and then think about my future. I might do an MBA here at the New International. What do you think? I phoned my father last night and told him about my plans. He didn't like the idea. He wants me to work in his business!

Bye,

C

Dear Kitty,

How are you? We had our farewell party today. It was so sad. I didn't say goodbye to everyone. I just left! I'm coming to see you soon. I'm going to spend a couple of months with my mum and dad. Did I tell you about the teacher training course? I'm starting in September. There's so much news. I'll give you a call in a week or so – as soon as I've settled in at home.

Love,

Language in Focus

Thinking about grammar
The future with the present continuous

We use the present continuous to talk about plans for the future.

1 **Complete these sentences with the present continuous form of the verbs** *take, stay, fly, go* **and** *get.*

a) Rosa _____ to London in the morning, isn't she?

b) I _____ a course in information technology in the summer.

c) Lee and Julia _____ married next month.

d) You _____ here next year, aren't you?

e) In March we _____ to Egypt for a holiday.

2 **Read the five notes and messages on page 127 again. Underline examples of the present continuous.**

3 **These people have plans. Write sentences about them using the present continuous. For example:**

Martin/Jakarta/Tuesday

Martin is flying to Jakarta on Tuesday.

Anita/tennis/tomorrow afternoon

_____

José and Beatríz/party/22nd June

Igor/his dacha/next week

Mandy/around the world/next winter

The future with *going to*

We also talk about plans using going to:

subject	is/are	going to	verb	
Jack	is	going	be	late.
You	are	to	pass	the exam.

Is/Are	subject	going to	verb	
Is	Maria	going	get	a job?
Are	they	to	see	a film?

4 **Put these words in order to make sentences.**

a) car/to/month/buy/Carlo/a/going/next/is/new

b) stay/with/summer/parents/you/to/the/are/going/your/in ?

c) increase/going/year/think/are/that/next/we/sales/to

d) weeks/Australia/in/going/visit/few/a/Yuki/to/is

e) be/Lee/accountant/banker/an/a/going/or/to/is ?

The future with *will*

We also talk about the future using the modal *will* (or *'ll*).

5 **Read these examples and complete the tables below.**

a) I'll speak to Hari later.

b) When will you see Anita?

c) It won't rain tomorrow.

d) Samia will go home at eight.

e) You won't forget, will you?

f) The economy will improve before the end of the year.

g) Will you stay in China next year?

h) Martha will be very happy when she hears the news.

I		speak	to Hari later.
Samia			home at eight.
The economy	will	improve	
Martha			very happy when she hears the news.

Negatives

It		rain	
You			will you?

Questions

When				Anita?
	Will	you		in China next year?

Expressing hopes, wishes and dreams

I'd (really) like/love to …   I hope to …

I want to …   I have an ambition to …

for a start   one day

as soon as possible/as soon as I can

and then   after that   eventually

 Discuss your life hopes, plans and ambitions with a partner. Use the language in the box above.

Listening

 Listen to Suzie and Janet talking about their hopes for the future. Complete the dialogue with these words and phrases:

> I hope to   as soon as   until later
> going to   I want to   Eventually
> one day   I'd like to   I suppose
> you know   really   I'd love to
> ambition   should

S: Here's your coffee, Janet. What are you thinking about? You look serious.

J: Nothing. Well, life, ① _____.

S: Life!

J: Well, my future really. I was 22 last week, ② _____.

S: Of course I know. We had a party, didn't we? But you're not old.

J: I know, but there are so many things ③ _____ do with my life.

S: Such as?

J: For a start, ④ _____ get a good job – ⑤ _____ I finish my course.

S: Me too. But it's not so easy.

J: And also ⑥ _____ travel. There are so many places I ⑦ _____ want to visit – Japan, Africa, Mexico …

S: I think you ⑧ _____ do that before you start to work!

J: And then ⑨ _____ get married and have a family ⑩ _____.

S: I'm ⑪ _____ leave all of that ⑫ _____.

J: And I have another ⑬ _____.

S: What's that?

J: To climb mountains – high mountains. ⑭ _____, I plan to climb Mount Everest.

S: Everest! Good heavens! Let's have some more coffee.

Skills in Focus – listening and speaking

Listening

 1 Sarah is interviewing Professor Norman from the Maths Department for Campus Radio. Listen to the interview and decide if the following statements are true or false.

a) Professor Norman came to the university five years ago.

b) He was born in Manchester in the United Kingdom.

c) He went to university in Manchester.

d) He finished his studies in 1995.

e) He found Maths easy at school.

f) His first job was in Singapore.

g) He got married while he was working in Singapore.

h) He worked in a university in Beijing for two years.

i) He didn't like China very much.

j) From China he came to the New International University.

k) He became a professor last year.

l) He plans to stay in Alumnia for a long time.

2 Now correct the false sentences.

Role play

 3 **Student A:** Choose a famous actor/actress. Find out information about his or her life and make notes.

Student B: Choose a famous singer. Find out information about his or her life and make notes.

4 **Student A:**

a) You are a famous actor/actress. Use your notes to answer your partner's questions.

b) Now interview your partner. He/She is a famous singer. Ask about his/her early life, what he/she is doing now and his/her plans for the future.

Student B:

a) Interview your partner. He/She is a famous actor/actress. Ask about his/her early life, what he/she is doing now and his/her plans for the future.

b) You are a famous singer. Use your notes to answer your partner's questions.

 5 Prepare a short talk about the famous person you interviewed. Give the talk to a small group or the whole class.

Skills in Focus – reading and writing

1 Reading

Discuss in a group.

a) What exciting or dangerous pastimes can you think of? Why do people like these activities?

b) Would you like to go on a short trip into space? Why/why not? Do you think that many people would like to be space tourists?

2 Read the newspaper article about space tourism quickly and find the answers to these questions.

a) Which company is organising the tours?

b) When will the first flight be?

c) How long does the trip last?

d) How long will the passengers be in space?

e) Do passengers need to be in excellent health?

3 Work with a partner. Discuss:

a) how the spacecraft will get into space.

b) what the passengers will experience in space.

c) Dennis Tito's trip and how it was different.

d) what the four-day training and preparation course will include.

4 Find out the meaning of the underlined words and expressions.

Space Trips – Just $100,000

Tourists could soon be travelling into space for a trip lasting between 60 and 90 minutes. Already 100 people, ranging in age from 18 to 76, have paid their <u>deposit</u> of $6,000 each to reserve a place.

An American company, Space Adventures, and Russian designers are offering the trips to those tourists who want something a little different. "Some people like the <u>thrill</u> of taking a risk, for example bungee jumpers and racing-car drivers," said Robert Haltermann, an expert in space tourism. "Some people like <u>to live on the edge</u>."

The first flight will probably be in the year 2005. A large Russian carrier plane, an M-55, will carry the small spacecraft to a height of 18 kilometres. The spacecraft, which holds only three people, will then <u>detach</u> from the plane. A pilot will switch on the rocket engine and take the two passengers to a height of more than 90 kilometres.

For five magical minutes the rocket will be outside the Earth's atmosphere. Passengers will experience zero gravity. They will see the blackness of space and the Earth <u>shining</u> far below.

Yesterday a model of the spacecraft, known as C-XXI, went on display at an air base near Moscow. One of the first to sign up was a Japanese doctor, Shuichi Okubo. "I hope to be one of the first to travel," he told reporters.

The first space tourist was Dennis Tito, an American millionaire. He paid a lot more, $20 million, for his two-day trip into deep space, organised by the same company. He went up in a Russian rocket and <u>boarded</u> a space station that <u>orbits</u> the Earth continuously – 400 kilometres into space.

For a trip into deep space, like Tito's trip, astronauts need to be in excellent health and spend months in preparation. But what about this short five-minute trip outside the Earth's atmosphere? An organiser said, "Passengers only need to be in fair health. They will <u>require</u> just four days of preparation and training."

Writing

5. You are going to be a passenger on a space trip. Write a letter to a close friend or family member explaining why you are going on the trip. Describe what you want to see and what you hope to experience.

6. Work in pairs. Design an advertisement for the trip. Give the necessary information. Try to persuade people to sign up.

Amazing Offer!
Journey of a lifetime

Study Tip Take an active part in discussions – but don't dominate!

... and another thing!

Discussions are an important part of study. They help you think more clearly about your views. Here are some tips for a good discussion:

Preparation for the discussion

- Learn about the subject for discussion.
- Make a note of what you want to say.
- Think about the opposite points of view.

During the discussion

- Listen to others.
- Express your views clearly.
- Don't dominate (but don't be silent).
- Disagree politely.
- Accept the views of other people politely.
- Be willing to learn.

Discussion

1. In a group, choose one of the following topics for discussion:
   - Modern architecture is ugly.
   - Space exploration is a waste of money.
   - Everyone should go to university.
   - Fast food is a danger to health.
   - Professional sportspeople are greedy.

   Prepare for the discussion using the tips above.

2. Have the discussion.

3. At the end, check your contribution. Did you follow the points above?

Vocabulary Review

Verbs and nouns

1 Complete the table. Use your dictionary to help you.

verb	noun
graduate	
	insurance
arrange	
	deposit
fly	
	experience
prepare	
discuss	
	information

2 Put these nouns in the table below. Try to put three nouns in each column. (Some nouns can go in more than one column.)

a plan   a decision   a family   a trip
an ambition   a journey   a tour
arrangements   a mistake

to go on	to have	to make

Task 1: Write three sentences using the phrases above.

Space travel

3 Draw a spidergram for *space travel*. Use these words and others that you know: *spacecraft, gravity, orbit ...*

Grammar Review

- **The future with the present continuous.**

We use the present continuous for plans in the future.

Lee **is flying** to Singapore in three weeks.

I**'m playing** tennis tomorrow afternoon.

- **The future with *going to***

Jack **is going to** be late.

Don't worry, you **are going to** pass the exam.

Is Maria **going to** get a job?

Are they **going to** see the film?

Task 2: Write six things you are planning to do next week. Use *going to*.

- **The future with *will***

We also talk about the future using the modal *will* (or *'ll*).

I **will** speak to Hari.

He **will** go home at 8.

She **will** be very happy.

Negatives

We **won't** have a party this year.

I **won't** be late.

Questions

Will they believe her?

Will we see you again soon?

Language Review

- **Expressing hopes, wishes and dreams**

I'd (really) like/love to ...

I hope to ...

I want to ...

I have an ambition to ...

for a start

as soon as possible/as soon as I can

and then

after that

one day

eventually

Task 3: Write a dialogue between two friends discussing their hopes for the future.

REVIEW UNIT C

Listening: Part 1

Write the missing words in the mini-dialogues, then listen to check your answers.

A

A: _____ _____ ask you for some advice?

B: Yes, _____ _____ . What is it?

A: Do you think I _____ _____ a new computer, or just increase the memory on my old one?

B: _____ _____ me! I don't know anything about computers!

B

A: Excuse me. Could you _____ _____ _____ some change for the car park?

B: I'm sorry. I _____ _____ . I haven't got any myself.

C

A: I'd like _____ _____ a double room, please.

B: _____ , madam. When for?

A: April 1ˢᵗ.

B: And for how _____ nights?

A: Three. We'll be leaving _____ _____ 4ᵗʰ.

B: Could you _____ _____ your credit card details, please?

A: Yes, _____ _____ . It's a visa card …

D

A: Hello?

B: Good evening. _____ _____ Reception.

A: Yes?

B: Sorry to disturb you. What time _____ _____ _____ your wake-up call in the morning?

A: 7.00 a.m., please. And could I _____ _____ breakfast in my room?

B: Certainly, sir. What would you like _____ _____ ?

A: Um. Coffee, orange juice …

E

A: Could I book _____ _____ from London to Manchester, please?

B: Yes, sir. When would you like _____ _____?

A: July 3ʳᵈ, please. I'd _____ to travel early morning, if possible.

B: _____ _____ our 7.15 a.m. flight is full, but we have another at 9.30.

A: What time _____ _____ _____?

B: That one _____ _____ 11.05.

A: That's too late. I _____ _____ there for a meeting _____ 10.30. I'll try another airline.

B: Sorry we can't help you, sir.

Listening: Part 2

7.05 p.m. Ecology Matters

A weekly programme that looks at 'green' ideas for a safer, cleaner planet. This week, interviewer Hilary Martin talks to the editor of *Green World* magazine about windmills.

You are going to listen to part of an interview for a radio programme called *Ecology Matters*.

2 Read the list below, then listen and tick the topics discussed in the interview.

☐ the history of windmills

☐ advantages and disadvantages of modern wind turbines

☐ advantages and disadvantages of different types of energy

☐ the future of wind turbines and wind power

☐ the history of water mills and water power

☐ the weather

3 Listen again and decide if the sentences below are true (T) or false (F).

a) Windmills are about 1,500 years old. ( )

b) People started using windmills in Europe about 1,000 years ago. ( )

c) About 200 years ago, windmills started to become less popular. ( )

d) Today we need to find different, cleaner types of power. ( )

e) Everybody thinks wind turbines are a good idea. ( )

f) Dave hopes there will be fewer wind turbines in future. ( )

g) Modern wind turbines can cause pollution. ( )

4 Complete the questions with the missing words, then listen and check your answers.

a) _____ _____ the first people to use windmills?

b) _____ _____ people _____ windmills for?

c) What _____ those?

d) So why _____ industry _____ windmills again?

e) And wind _____ a continuous resource, _____ it?

f) So _____ _____ it _____ so long to change to wind power for our electricity?

g) Why _____?

h) And _____ _____ their 'true beauty' exactly?

Reading and study skills

5 Read the text. Find one grammatical mistake in each fact and correct it.

Did you know ...?

10 facts you didn't know about **wind power**

- The UK is the windy place in Europe and has 40 per cent of Europe's best sites for wind farms. But the UK is behind other European countries in building them.

- Denmark get 15 per cent of its power from the wind.

- The UK only gets three per cent of its power from wind turbine.

- The UK government has promised that 10 per cent of the UKs power will come from the wind by 2010.

- The world's large wind turbine is in Hawaii. It has two 50-metre long blades on top of a tower. It is as tall as a 20-storey building.

- On a wind farm in California there are 300 wind generators. They drive turbines that are connected to an electricity generator. They can collecting enough energy to light and heat a small town.

- On average we 'get back' the energy we use to build a wind turbine in three to four months of operation. One 600-kilowatt turbine can provide enough electric for 400 homes.

- Scientists estimates that by 2030, wind power will provide more than 10 per cent of the world's electricity.

- A windiest place in the world is Antarctica. The winds often blow at 320 km/h.

- The strongest wind ever recorded were 371 km/h at Mount Washington, in New Hampshire, United States, on 12 April, 1934.

6 Read the text and complete each sentence below with the correct number.

a) _____ of Europe's best windmill sites are in the UK.

b) The quantity of the UK's power coming from the wind will be _____ by the year 2010.

c) Each blade on the Hawaiian wind turbine is _____ long.

d) _____ wind generators can provide a small town with electricity.

e) It only takes _____ months to replace the energy we need to build a wind turbine.

f) A _____ turbine is all we need for 400 homes to have electricity.

g) In the year _____, 10 per cent of all our electricity will come from the wind.

h) In Antarctica, the average wind speed is _____ .

Writing

7 Write what you know about the history of water power, the advantages and disadvantages of water power, and possible future uses. (75 words)

_____

_____

_____

_____

_____

_____

_____

_____

_____

_____

Vocabulary

8 Add five more words or phrases to each column in the table.

hotels	airports	sightseeing	jobs
waiter	aisle seat	go on a boat trip	apply for

9 Find the odd word out in each list. You will need to think carefully about the different parts of speech for each word.

Example:

improve/arrange/accept/govern

Accept is different from the other verbs, because the noun form is *acceptance*. All the others have the ending -*ment* in their noun forms: improve**ment**, arrange**ment**, govern**ment**.

a) attraction/enthusiasm/fantasy/science

b) qualify/translate/motivate/serve

c) understanding/comfort/probability/danger

d) memory/visual/insurance/speciality

e) imagine/beautify/respect/succeed/forget

f) concentrate/accept/prepare/apply/inform

WORD LIST

Abbreviations used in this word list:
adj = adjective
adv = adverb
conj = conjunction
count = countable
exp = expression
n = noun
plur = plural
uncount = uncountable
v = verb

Unit 1

academy (n)
accommodation (n)
actually (adv)
address (n)
administration (n)
afternoon (n)
again (adv)
arts (plur n)
as well as (conj)
at the end of (prep)
at the moment (exp)
athletics (n)

basketball (n)
beautiful (adj)
before (conj)
behind (prep)
belong (v)
between (prep)
block (n)
bookshop (n)
brain (n)
building (n)
business studies (n)

cafeteria (n)
campus (n)
canteen (n)
capital (n)
car park (n)
centre (n)
certificate (n)
chat (v, chatting, chatted)
choose (v, choosing, chose)
city (n)
clock (n)
clocktower (n)
college (n)
come in (v, coming, came)
computer (n)
computer laboratory (n)
countryside (n)
course (n, academic –)
court (n, basketball –, tennis –)

dean (n)
degree (n)
department (n)
description (n)
different (adj)
diploma (n)

direction (n)

education (n)
e-mail (n)
engineering (n)
enough (adj)
entrance (n)
entry (n)
evening (n)

facility (n)
faculty (n)
family (n)
first (adj)
floor (n)
foreign (adj)
formal (adj)
fountain (n)
friendly (adj)

glad (adj)
great (adj)
greeting (n)
ground floor (n)
guard (n)
gymnasium (n)

hall (n)
headline (n)
hear (v, hearing, heard)
help (v)
high (adj)

important (adj)
in front of (prep)
in the middle (prep)
in touch with (exp)
informal (adj)
information (n)
information technology (n)
institute (n)
instruction (n)
introduce (v)
introduction (n)

jeep (n)

kilometre (n)

language (n)
large (adj)
law (n)
lecture hall (n)
lecturer (n)
level (n)
library (n)
like (v)
located (adj)
location (n)
look for (v)
lovely (adj)

main (adj)
map (n)
maths (n)
medical (adj)

medicine (n)
medium (n)
message (n)
millennium (n)
miss (v)
modern (adj)
month (n)
morning (n)

near (prep)
need (v)
news (plur n)
next to (prep)
nice (adj)

offer (v)
office (n)
on the left (prep)
on the right (prep)
on top of (prep)
open (v)
opposite (prep)
order (n)
outside (prep)
over there (adv)
overseas (adj)

part (n)
physics (n)
picture (n)
pitch (n football –)
place (n)
point (n)
professor (n)
prospectus (n)

qualification (n)

registration (n)
reply (v, replying, replied)

science (n)
secretary (n)
see (v, seeing, saw)
sit (v, sitting, sat)
small (adj)
snack bar (n)
soon (adv)
southwest (adj)
speak (v, speaking, spoke)
staff (n)
standard (n)
start (v)
stay (v)
storey (n)
sure (adj)
swimming pool (n)

tennis (n)
test (n)
toilets (n)
track (n)
training centre (n)

university (n)

visit (v)
visitor (n)

website (n)
week (n)
west (n)
wife (n)
wish (n)

year (n)

Unit 2

access (n)
accounting (n)
accurate (adj)
accurately (adv)
across (prep)
add (v)
advice (n)
afraid (adj)
agree (v)
air-conditioning (n)
alarm (n)
analogue (adj)
ancient (adj)
arrange (v)
article (n)
atomic (adj)

barrel (n)
battery (n)
be able to (v)
become (v, becoming, became)
belt (n)
body (n)
bowl (n)
business management (n)
busy (adj)

calendar (n)
call (n)
carry (v)
cassette (n)
chemistry (n)
coffee (n)
cold (n)
computer studies (n)
connect (v)
crystal (n)

date (n)
design (v)
dial (n)
dictionary (n)
digital (adj)
divide (v)

economics (n)
energy (n)
enjoy (v)
equal (adj)
escape (v)
exam (n)

expensive (adj)

fall (v, falling, fell)
fashion (n)
finance (n)
fix (v)
float (n)
free (adj)
French (n)
Friday (n)
full (adj)
function (n)
future (n)

geography (n)
glass (n, uncount)
grammar (n)

half (n, plur *halves*)
hand (n)
heat (n)
help (n)
hole (n)
holiday (n)
hour (n)
hourglass (n)

idea (n)
indicate (v)
inside (prep)
instrument (n)
Internet (n)
Internet site (n)
item (n)

jewellery (n)
journal (n)

language lab (n)
leather (n)
like (prep)
list (n)
lunch break (n)
lunchtime (n)

magazine (n)
mark (n)
marketing (n)
mathematics (n)
measure (v)
meet (v, meeting, met)
meeting (n)
midday (n)
middle (n)
midnight (n)
mobile phone (n)
Monday (n)

noisy (adj)
number (n)

October (n)
organise (v)

phone (v)
plan (n)

plastic (n)
pocket (n)
possible (adj)
power (n)
practice (n)
private (adj)
problem (n)

quarter (n)
quartz (n)
quiet (adj)

really (adv)
reference book (n)
relax (v)
resource (n)
rest (v)
rise (v, rising, rose)

sand (n)
Saturday (n)
second (n)
shadow (n)
shape (n)
side (n)
simple (adj)
sky (n)
sometimes (adv)
Spanish (n)
stopwatch (n)
strap (n)
study (n)
subject (n)
summer (n)
Sunday (n)
sundial (n)
surface (n)

tea (n)
tell the time (v, telling, told)
third (adj)
through (prep)
Thursday (n)
timetable (n)
tiny (adj)
tomorrow (adj)
Tuesday (n)
turn over (v)
tutor (n)

unlike (prep)
until (prep)

vertical (adj)
vibrate (v)
video (n)
volleyball (n)

watch (n)
way (n)
wear (v, wearing, wore)
Wednesday (n)
weekly (adj)
winter (n)
world (n)
wristwatch (n)

Unit 3

above (prep)
advantage (n)
air (n)
anywhere (adv)
apartment (n)
apple (n)
apple pie (n)
around (prep)

banana (n)
bank (n)
basic (adj)
Bedouin (n)
bedroom (n)
beef (n)
biscuit (n)
brother (n)
build (v, building, built)
burger (n)

cake (n)
caravan (n)
central heating (n)
cheese (n)
chicken (n)
Chinese (n)
chocolate (n)
clinic (n)
cola (n)
cold (adj)
company (n)
cook (v)
cottage (n)
countable (adj)
country (n)
cup (n)
customer (n)

delicious (adj)
delight (n)
desert (n)
dessert (n)
disadvantage (n)
drink (n and v, drinking, drank)
during (prep)

east (n)
eat (v, eating, ate)
egg (n)
exercise (n)
expression (n)

factory (n)
farm (n)
flat (n)
food (n)
forest (n)
french fries (n)
fresh (adj)
frost (n)
fruit (n)

garden (n)
girl (n)
girlfriend (n)
glass (n, count)
goat (n)
grandparent (n)
grey (adj)
grow (v, growing, grew)
Gypsy (n)

hair (n)
happy (adj)
hard (adj)
heart (n)
home (n)
hot (adj)
however (conj)
hundred (n)
hungry (adj)

ice-cream (n)
in order to (conj)

Japanese (n)
job (n)
juice (n)
just a minute (exp)

lake (n)
leave (v, leaving, left)
leg (n)
lemonade (n)

Malay (n)
madam (n)
manager (n)
menu (n)
milk (n)
milkshake (n)
mug (n)
multinational (adj)
mushroom (n)

normally (adv)
north (n)

oil (n)
open (adj)
orange (n)
order (v)
owner (n)

parent (n)
philosophy (n)
piece (n)
pizza (n)
Portuguese (n)
prepare (v)
product (n)
project (n)
protection (n)

relative (n)
remember (v)
repair (v)
request (v)

researcher (n)
restaurant (n)
return (v)
rice (n)
river (n)
road (n)
rule (n)
Russian (adj)

salad (n)
sandwich (n)
scientific (adj)
seat (n)
sell (v, selling, sold)
send (v, sending, sent)
share (v)
sheep (n)
shop (n)
show (v)
sister (n)
sleep (v, sleeping, slept)
snack (n)
snow (n)
spend (v, time, spending, spent)
spring (n)
strawberry (n)
suburb (n)
sweet (adj)
swim (v, swimming, swam)

tall (adj)
temperature (n)
tent (n)
thirsty (adj)
town (n)
traffic (n)
travel (v, travelling, travelled)
tropical (adj)
tuna (n)

uncountable (adj)
understand (v, understanding, understood)
unfortunately (adv)
Urdu (n)
usually (adv)

vanilla (n)
vegetable (n)
village (n)

waiter (n)
walk (v)
warm (adj)
wash (v)
whole (adj)
wooden (adj)
work (n and v)

yoghurt (n)

Unit 4

admire (v)
aeroplane (n)

Africa (n)
airport (n)
America (n)
American (adj)
animal (n)
architecture (n)
Asia (n)
ask for (v)
attraction (n)
attractive (adj)
Australasia (n)

backpack (n)
bag (n)
baggage reclaim (n)
bar chart (n)
bargain (n)
beach (n)
boat (n)
bottle (n)
box (n)
Brazil (n)
breakfast (n)
briefcase (n)
British (adj)
brochure (n)

camping (n)
carpet (n)
castle (n)
CD (n)
chair (n)
chart (n)
cheap (adj)
check (v)
check-in (n)
cigarette (n)
climate (n)
close (v)
coast (n)
colourful (adj)
continent (n)
cool (adj)
cool-box (n)
crowd (n)
customs (n)
customs officer (n)

definition (n)
dollar (n)
dozen (n)
down (prep)
dramatic (adj)
dry (adj)
duty free (n)

economical (adj)
eighth (adj)
elegant (adj)
Equator (n)
Europe (n)
exciting (adj)
exit (n)
explore (v)

famous (adj)

feel (v, feeling, felt)
fifth (adj)
figure (n)
fish (n)
flight (n)
fort (n)
fourth (adj)
France (n)

gold (n)
ground (n)
guidebook (n)

handbag (n)
harbour (n)
historic (adj)
history (n)
hospitable (adj)
hotel (n)

immigration (n)
increase (n)
interesting (adj)
international (adj)
Ireland (n)
island (n)
Italy (n)

Jamaica (n)
Japan (n)
join (v)
jungle (n)

Kenya (n)
kilo (n)

lift (n)
lobster (n)
local (adj)
luggage (n)

market (n)
meal (n)
meanwhile (adv)
metre (n)
million (n)
money (n)
mountain (n)
museum (n)

ninth (adj)

ocean (n)
organisation (n)

park (n)
passport (n)
perfume (n)
photo (n)
picnic (n)
picturesque (adj)
plain (n)
planet (n)
pleasant (adj)
political (adj)
popular (adj)

population (n)
port (n)
position (n)
present (n)
pretty (adj)
pronunciation (n)
public (adj)
publish (v)

rain (n)
region (n)
religious (adj)
represent (v)

scene (n)
scenery (n)
sea level (n)
second (adj)
sense (n)
September (n)
seventh (adj)
shop (v)
shopper (n)
sight (n)
sign (n)
sixth (adj)
sleeping bag (n)
Spain (n)
spare (adj)
springs (n)
square (n)
stand (v, standing, stood)
storm (n)
stove (n)
street (n)
suit (v)
suitcase (n)
sunshine (n)
surprise (n)

taste (n)
tenth (adj)
Thailand (n)
throughout (prep)
ticket (n)
title (n)
torch (n)
total (n)
tourism (n)
tourist (n)
traditional (adj)
transport (n)
trip (n)

United States (n, the —)

valley (n)
vehicle (n)
view (n)
viewing platform (n)

wild (adj)
wonderful (adj)

Unit 5

advertisement (n)
afford (v)
ahead (adv)
along (prep)
amazing (adj)
argument (n)

balcony (n)
better (adj)
blackboard (n)
bookshelf (n, plur *bookshelves*)

calculate (v)
calculator (n)
carefully (adv)
cassette recorder (n)
century (n)
chance (n)
cinema (n)
collocate (v)
collocation (n)
condition (n)
convert (v)
copy (v)
correct (v)
correction (n)
corridor (n)
cost (v, costing, cost)
criminal (n)
crossroad (n)
cupboard (n)
currency (n)

database (n)
dedicated (adj)
delivery (n)
desk (n)
diagram (n)
diamond (n)
digit (n)

electricity (n)
electronic (adj)
encyclopaedia (n)
equation (n)
equip (v)
essay (n)
examiner (n)
expert (n)

feature (n)
flat (adj)
follow (v)
fun (n)

garage (n)
gate (n)
give (v, giving, gave)
graph (n)

hardware (n)
health (n)

hostel (n)

ideal (adj)
indoor (adj)
instant (adj)
instantly (adv)
interview (n)

journey (n)

key (n)

laptop (n, – computer)
late (adj)
long (adj)
look forward to (v)

machine (n)
method (n)

neighbour (n)
network (n)

pass (v, – the time)
plant (n)
plot (v, plotting, plotted)
pocket-sized (adj)
policeman (n)
press (v)
price (n)
print (v)
printer (n)

quote (n)

object (n)

rainy (adj)
roof (n)
root (n)
row (n)

satellite dish (n)
season (n)
shade (n)
size (n)
smoke (v)
specialise (v)
speed (n)
spell (v, spelling, spelt)
spellchecker (n)
sports hall (n)
stop (v, stopping, stopped)
store (v)
straight (adv)
sum (n)
supplier (n)
switch (n)
system (n)

text (n)
thesaurus (n)
turning (n)
type (v)

useful (adj)

visual (n)

wait (v)
wall (n)
whiteboard (n)
window (n)
worry (v)

Unit 6

area (n)
art gallery (n)
atmosphere (n)
autumn (n)
average (adj)

big (adj)
billion (n)
bitterly (adv)
Brazilian (n)
bus station (n)

capacity (n)
Chinese (adj)
commercial (adj)
committee (n)
compare (v)
context (n)
cost (n)
covered (adj)

dam (n)
daughter (n)
district (n)
drop (v, dropping, dropped)
dynasty (n)

economic (adj)
economy (n)
enormous (adj)

far (adj)
few (adj)
film (n)
financial (adj)
flatten (v)
form (n, question –)
found (v)

handle (v)
hat (n)
heavy (adj)
hometown (n)
hospital (n)
humid (adj)
humidity (n)

ill (adj)
increasing (adj)
industrial (adj)
Indian (adj)
Indonesia (n)
industry (n)

kitchen (n)

land (n and v)
light (adj)
link (n)

mainland (n)
manufacturing (n)
many (adj)
mild (adj)
misunderstand (v, misunderstanding, misunderstood)
more (adj)
motorway (n)

natural (adj)
near (adj)
new (adj)

old (adj)
Olympic Games (n)
oxygen (n)

passenger (n)
president (n)
propose (v)
prosperous (adj)
province (n)

railway (n)
railway station (n)
rich (adj)
roundabout (n)
runway (n)

satellite (n)
semester (n)
short (adj)
situation (n)
snowy (adj)
solution (n)
son (n)
space (n)
span (n)
Spanish (adj)
stadium (n)
stupid (adj)
sufficient (adj)
sunny (adj)
suspension bridge (n)

temple (n)
textile (n)
tower (n)

ugly (adj)
unattractive (adj)

weather (n)
wet (adj)
wind (n)
windy (adj)
worse (adj)

young (adj)
yours faithfully (exp)

Unit 7

abbreviation (n)
aloud (adv)
amount (n)
annoy (v)
appear (v)
appliance (n)
application (n)
arrow (n)
art (n)
attach (v)

bank account (n)
bar code (n)
bill (n)
borrow (v)
bottom (n)
button (n)

calculation (n)
card (n)
circle (n)
clear (adj)
click (v)
code (n)
concert (n)
congratulations (n)
control (v, controlling, controlled)
cricket (n)
cut (v, cutting, cut)

dangerous (adj)
data (n)
disk (n)
display (v)
document (n)
drag (v, dragging, dragged)

engine (n)
equipment (n)

fast (adj)
file (n)

goods (n)
graphics (n)
guide (v)

hairdresser (n)
handle (n)

icon (n)
imaginary (adj)
instructor (n)
intelligent (adj)

jacket (n)

keep (v, – a record, keeping, kept)
keep (v, – in touch, keeping, kept)
keyboard (n)

man-made (adj)

matter (n)
mirror (n)
modem (n)
monitor (n)
motorbike (n)
mouse (n, computing)

need (n)

ordinary (adj)·

paint (v)
paste (v)
percentage (n)
photograph (n)
point (v)
prefer (v)
produce (v)
program (n)

rat (n)
receive (v)
recently (adv)
record (n)
repeat (v)
repetitive (adj)
reply (n)
rocket (n)
run (v, running, ran)

save (v)
scientist (n)
select (v)
shopkeeper (n)
slow (adj)
snail (n)
solve (v)
sound (n)
speaker (n)
stone (n)
studio (n)
supermarket (n)
survey (n)
switch on (v)

task (n)

video recorder (n)

wake (someone) up (v, waking, woke)
writing (n)

Unit 8

angry (adj)
apology (n)
arm (n)
astronaut (n)

basically (adv)
booking (n)
bored (adj)
buy (v, buying bought)

143

caller (n)
camera (n)
certainly (adv)
clean (v)
clearly (adv)
communicate (v)
communication (n)
communicative (adj)
communicator (n)
conference (n)

diary (n)
doctor (n)
drive (v, driving, drove)
duty (n)

early (adj)
educated (adj)
electronics (n)
event (n)

face (n)
face-to-face (adj)
fax (n)
fax machine (n)
feedback (n)
filing cabinet (n)
finish (v)
fluently (adv)

German (n)
greet (v)

hold (v, holding, held)
horse (n)

improve (v)
interested (adj)
interview (v)

journalism (n)

letter (n)
line (n)
lucky (adj)

match (n, football –)
mechanic (n)
memo (n)
ministry (n)

newspaper (n)
notepad (n)
notice board (n)
novel (n)

official (adj)
opinion (n)

paperclip (n)
personal (adj)
photocopier (n)
photocopy (n and v)
pie chart (n)
plenty (n)
poem (n)

positive (adj)
presentation (n)
put (someone) through (v, putting, put)

race (n)
read (v, reading, read)
receiver (n)
receptionist (n)
regular (adj)
report (n)

sales (n)
salesman (n)
secondly (adv)
service (v)
shoe (n)
sick (adj)
singer (n)
stapler (n)
switch off (v)

tour guide (n)
typical (adj)

upset (adj)

washing machine (n)
writer (n)

Unit 9

adventure (n)
aerobics (n)
astronomy (n)
athlete (n)
avalanche (n)
awful (adj)

billiards (n)
bowling (n)
breeze (n)
bungee jumping (n)

canyon (n)
carry out (v)
cause (v)
challenge (n)
champion (n)
cliff (n)
climbing (n)
cloud (n)
cloudy (adj)
club (n)
coin (n)
connector (n)
couple (n)
curved (adj)
cycling (n)
cyclone (n)

damage (n)
danger (n)
dark (adj)
dense (adj)

destruction (n)
develop (v)
dislike (n)

earthquake (n)
eventually (adv)
eye (n)
extremely (adv)

factor (n)
fairly (adv)
favourite (adj)
fire (n)
flood (n)
following (adj)
force (v)
form (n, application –)
form (v)
freezing (adj)
frozen (adj)

gardening (n)
get up (v, getting, got)

hailstorm (n)
hate (v)
healthy (adj)
heavily (adv)
hobby (n)
horse riding (n)
hot chocolate (n)
housework (n)
hurricane (n)

indoors (adj)
intonation (n)

jogging (n)

karate (n)

like (n)
lose (v, losing, lost)
loud (adj)
love (v)

marathon (n)
melt (v)
mix (v)
moment (n)
musical (adj)

noise (n)

occur (v, occurring, occurred)
outdoors (adj)
outline (n)

painter (n)
painting (n)
pastime (n)
path (n)
peak (n)
phenomena (plur n)
piano (n)
point (n, low –)

postcard (n)
pottery (n)
powerful (adj)
predict (v)
pressure (n)
property (n)

quite (adv)

radio (n)
range (n)
rap (n, – music)
rapidly (adv)
rather (adv)
reach (v)
recent (adj)
risk (n)
rock (n, – music)
rough (adj)
runner (n)

shipping (n)
shout (v)
signal (n)
skill (n)
sleep (n)
snow (v)
stable (adj)
stamp collecting (n)
strength (n)
stucture (n)
sudden (adj)
surf (v)

team (n)
technical college (n)
tidal wave (n)
toast (n)
tornado (n)
traffic jam (n)
train (v)
type (n)
typhoon (n)

umbrella (n)
upwards (adv)

vibration (n)

Unit 10

aim (at) (v)
always (adv)
ammunition (n)
appointment (n)
arrival (n)
artistic (adj)

band (n)
battlefield (n)
bow (v)
bucket (n)

cartoon (n)

cheek (n)
cloth (n)
colleague (n)
comfortable (adj)
crowd (v)
culture (n)
custom (n)

disappear (v)

earn (v)

festival (n)
finally (adv)
find out (v, finding, found)
fireworks (n)
first (adv)
first of all (exp)
flower (n)

garlic (n)
gather (v, intransitive)
greenery (n)
guest (n)

harvest festival (n)
hell (n)
highlighter (n)
honour (v)
host (n)
huge (adj)

imagine (v)
impolite (adj)
impromptu (adj)
inhospitable (adj)
intestines (n)
Iran (n)
Iranian (adj)

jeans (n)
join in (v)

kiss (v)

loaded (with) (adj)
lorry (n)

messy (adj)

national (adj)
necessary (adj)
never (n)

often (adv)
overcrowded (adj)

participate (v)
polite (adj)
punctual (adj)

remind (v)
resident (n)
rewrite (v, rewriting, rewrote)
ripe (adj)
routine (n)

rude (adj)

secular (adj)
serious (adj)
shake (hands) (v, shaking, shook)
sheet (n)
shoot (at) (v, shooting, shot)
silver (n)
soft (adj)
speciality (n)
spice (n)
squash (v)
squeeze (v)
stomach (n)
strange (adj)
stranger (n)

take place (v, taking, took)
target (n)
taxi (n)
textbook (n)
throw (v, throwing, threw)
tip (n)
tomato (n)
tonic (n)
T-shirt (n)
treat (v)
truck (n)

unfriendly (adj)
unimportant (adj)
unnecessary (adj)
unusual (adj)

vinegar (n)

war (n)

Unit 11

advertise (v)
anglophone (adj)
Arabic (n)
Argentina (n)
automatic (adj)

Berber (n)
bilingual (adj)
branch (n)
business (n)

Canada (n)
choice (n)
classification (n)
colony (n)
complete (v)
Cuba (n)
curve (n)

deal (n)
dentist (n)
dialect (n)
directly (adv)
Dutch (n)

English (n)

Farsi (n)

fluent (adj)
fortunately (adv)

government (n)
Greece (n)
Greek (n)

Hungarian (n)
Hungary (n)

install (software) (v)
interpreter (n)
Italian (n)

Korean (n)
Kuwait (n)

maximum (n)
minimum (n)
minority (n)
Mozambique (n)

native language (n)
Netherlands (n, the —)
Nigeria (n)
Norwegian (n)

pay (v)
Pakistan (n)
Philippines (n, the —)
politeness (n)
poster (n)
put an end (to) (exp)

Russian (n)

Senegal (n)
server (n)
sign (v)
software (n)
status (n)
step (n)
Sudan (n)
Swahili (n)
Sweden (n)
Swedish (n)

Taiwan (n)
Thai (n)
translation (n)
translator (n)
trust (v)
Tunisia (n)
Turkey (n)
Turkish (n)
turn down (v)

underline (v)
United Kingdom (n, the —)
urgent (adj)
verb (n)
vocabulary (n)

vowel (n)

widely (adv)

Yemen (n)

Unit 12

aisle (n)
arrive (v)
available (adj)

bar (n)
bathroom (n)
blow (v, blowing, blew)
board (v)
book (v)
business class (n)

cathedral (n)
check in (v)
chef (n)
cleanliness (n)
cockroach (n)
comfort (n)
contact (v)
continental breakfast (n)
convenient (adj)

depart (v)
departure (n)
dining room (n)
double room (n)

en suite (n, adj)

fare (n)

gate (n, airport departure —)

heaven (n)
hurt (v, hurting hurt)

install (a lift) (v)

lobby (n)
lounge (n)
luxury (n)

malaria (n)
mosque (n)

on-line (adv)

palace (n)
park (n)
plane (n)
porter (n)
prawn (n)

rate (n)
reasonable (adj)
reception (n)
reservation (n)

return (n, flight)
riyal (n)
room service (n)

serve (v)
sightsee (v – sightseeing, went sightseeing)
single room (n)
statue (n)
steak (n)
suite (n)

tour (n)
travel agent (n)

uncomfortable (adj)

Unit 13

accept (v)
accident (n)
advance (n)
advise (v)
apply (v)
aspirin (n)
associate (v)

bar (n, of a cage)
bother (v)
break down (v, breaking, broke)

cage (n)
climb (v)
company (n, uncount)
concentrate (v)

disease (n)
DNA (n)

effort (n)
enjoyment (n)
enthusiastic (adj)
experienced (adj)

fantastic (adj)
fantasy (n)
forget (v, forgetting, forgot)
formation (n)
furry (adj)

guess (v)

happiness (n)
homesick (adj)

image (n)
imitation (n)
in the first place (exp)
instrumental (adj)
intelligence (n)
intrinsic (adj)

keep (someone) going (exp)
leave behind (v, leaving, left)
long-term (adj)•

lottery (n)

managing director (n)
master (v)
memorise (v)
memory (n)
mental (adj)
molecular biology (n)
motivate (v)
motivation (n)
mouse (n, plur *mice*)

normal (adj)

ought (modal v)

part-time (adj)
pay attention (exp)
phone call (n)
pleasure (n)
psychologist (n)
psychology (n)

quality (n)

reaction (n)
reason (n)
recruit (v)
research (n)
respected (adj)
reward (n)

short-term (adj)
stomachache (n)
strong (adj)
successful (adj)

technology (n)

uncle (n)

visual (adj)
visualise (v)

Unit 14

aboard (adj)
absolutely (adv)
achieve (v)
achievement (n)
actor (n)
actress (n)
air force (n)
along with (exp)
ambassador (n)
arrogant (adj)
artist (n)
aside from (exp)

be born (—, was born)
biography (n)
brave (adj)
cadet (n)
can (n)

catch (v, catching, caught)
cobra (n)
collection (n)
consecutively (adv)
cosmonaut (n)
crash (n)

disagree (v)
distinction (n)
dragon (n)
dream (v)
dress (n)
dull (adj)

entertainer (n)
even though (conj)

fame (n)
fascinated (adj)
field (n)
film star (n)
former (adj)

get married (v, getting, got)
goal (n)
graduate (v)
growth (n)

handsome (adj)
hero (n)

invent (v)

kind (adj)

marry (v)
media (n)
model (n)
musician (n)

nowadays (exp)

obsession (n)
orbit (n)

pilot (n)
poisonous (adj)
politician (n)
politics (n)
profession (n)

radiation (n)
radioactive (adj)
rapid (adj)
real (adj)
reality show (n)
record-breaker (n)
rotate (v)
royalty (n)

score (v)
show (n)
skilful (adj)
snake (n)
soup (n)
spacecraft (n)

success (n)

talent (n)
term (n, scientific −)
terrible (adj)
tragically (adv)

win (v, winning, won)

Unit 15

accountant (n)
air base (n)
ambition (n)
arrangement (n)
as soon as (conj)
atmosphere (n)

banker (n)
blackness (n)
below (prep)

close (adj)
continuously (adv)

deposit (n)
designer (n)
detach (v)
diving (n)
dominate (v)

Earth (n)
edge (n)
excellent (adj)
experience (v)
exploration (n)

fair (adj)
farewell (n)
fast food (n)
fixed (adj)

go on display (exp)
Good heavens! (exp)
graduation (n)
gravity (n)

height (n)

insurance (n)

last (v)
lifetime (n)

magical (adj)
member (n)
Mexico (n)
millionaire (n)

note (n)

orbit (v)
organiser (n)

party (n)
persuade (v)
point of view (n)
preparation (n)
professional (adj)

racing car (n)
range (v)
reporter (n)
require (v)
reserve (v)

settle in (v)
shine (v, shining, shone)
sign up (v)

thrill (n)

waste (n)
wedding (n)
willing (adj)

zero (n)